PROPLINER
RENAISSANCE

Graham Robson

Airlife

Related titles published by Airlife

Vintage Aircraft over America
Geoff Jones and Chuck Stewart
Air to air photographs of US aircraft designed
between 1916 and 1961
ISBN 1 84037 296 6

Airlife's Classic Airliner Series
Boeing Stratocruiser ISBN 1 84037 242 7
Lockheed Constellation ISBN 1 84037 228 1

Colour Series
Airline Nostalgia ISBN 1 85310 951 7
Airliners of the 1960s ISBN 1 84037 124 2
American Classics of the Air ISBN 1 84037 106 4
Douglas DC-3 – The Survivors ISBN 1 84037 152 8
Douglas Propliners ISBN 1 84037 247 8
Faded Glory ISBN 1 84037 088 9
Piston Powered Propliners ISBN 1 84037 161 7
Shuttleworth Collection ISBN 1 84037 072 6

Copyright © 2002 Graham Robson

First published in the UK in 2002
by Airlife Publishing Ltd

British Library Cataloguing-in-Publication Data
A catalogue record for this book
is available from the British Library

ISBN 1 84037 274 5

Printed in Hong Kong

For details of other Airlife titles please contact:

Airlife Publishing Ltd
101 Longden Road, Shrewsbury, SY3 9EB, England
E-mail: sales@airlifebooks.com
Website: www.airlifebooks.com

CONTENTS

1 INTRODUCTION 4

2 THE EARLY YEARS 5

3 A CLASSIC . . . BY ANY OTHER NAME 19

4 DC-4 SKYMASTER 38

5 BIG TWINS 61

6 BEST OF BRITISH 83

7 HEAVY METAL 93

INDEX 112

INTRODUCTION

We have all marvelled at the rich selection of once rare and unusual types that now appear almost commonplace in the world of 'warbird' restorations. A well-established fraternity, supported by an equally well-established network of airframe, engine and systems experts, has blossomed to support the growing world-wide warbird movement. Now, a different, but equally dedicated and determined breed of owners and restorers is broadening the horizons of the aircraft enthusiast.

Two generations of airline passengers have now grown up never having known the experience of early air travel. The fabulously noisy and smoky engine-starts as the ageing propliner coughed and spluttered into life. Long flights in noisy and unpressurised cabins, the restricted cruising height that meant having to endure much of the flight 'in the weather', instead of cruising comfortably on top of it. The unmistakable and all-pervading smell of burnt oil and AvGas; all the suffering that was early air travel which, to many, is now fondly looked back on as a Golden Age.

This glorious experience is slowly being rediscovered by thousands of enthusiasts around the world, as more and more classic airliners and transports have new life breathed into them. The nostalgia of a past age has been brought back to life. Aircraft restoration, by definition, is a work of consummate dedication, patience, expense and above all, hard work. It is to the valued historians who undertake this work that this book is dedicated.

Prop Perfection was published four years ago, with the aim of illustrating some of the less-well-known, large-scale aircraft restorations, mostly with a military background. This follow-up volume is intended to redress the balance by depicting the growing number of privately owned and operated and beautifully restored Propliners. In photographing the aircraft featured, I have once again had the pleasure of meeting and getting to know many owners and their cherished mounts, each supported by an immeasurable army of dedicated volunteers intent on bringing a little bit of history back to life.

In chronicling the efforts of these dedicated individuals and groups, I have been assisted by a number of friends and fellow enthusiasts who very generously loaned pictures for inclusion. Particular thanks are due to Michael Prophet, Keith Gaskell, Jon Proctor, Martin Siegrest, Paul van den Berg, Paul van der Horst, Gordon Bain, Foe Geldersma, Eric Quenardel, Matthias Winkler and Gordon Reid, to whom I am most grateful.

Graham Robson

Surprisingly, pre-war types are fairly well represented in the world of restored airliners. The comparative lack of sophistication of these types does not make their restoration and operation any easier than the larger, post-war designs, however.

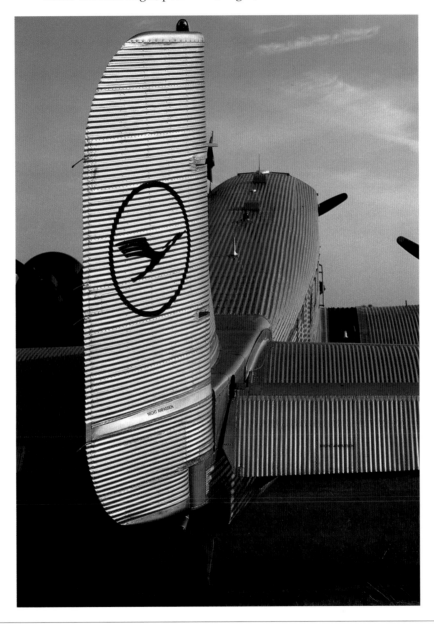

A pioneer in the development of an all-metal airliner was the German manufacturer Junkers, whose six-seat Junkers F13 flew soon after World War One, heralding a very successful family of similar types. Through this genesis, with designs increasing in size and capacity every time, the Ju-52 was eventually developed, in both single-and three-engined versions, with capacity for up to seventeen passengers. The type's outstanding characteristics and performance at that time soon resulted in its operation all over the world.

During fifteen years of manufacture the Ju-52 design altered little, from the original single-engined Ju-52/1m introduced in 1931 to the more common tri-motor variant. 'Iron Annie', as the type was affectionately dubbed, was operated in more than forty countries, flying commercially until the 1950s, with a number of air forces still flying home-produced versions of the Ju-52 until the early 1970s.

One of the most famous and well-travelled Ju-52s still flying is Lufthansa's superbly restored example *Tante Ju* (Aunt Ju). The German national airline is rightly proud of its Junkers and has shown it off in many countries, even crossing the Atlantic in 1990 on a 34-city tour of the United States, visiting all twelve of Lufthansa's gateway airports in that time.

The story of this fantastic restoration began in 1984 when the airline began searching for an example of the star of its pre-war fleet. The search took airline representatives to Florida, where a tired-looking example of Junkers' most famous design was based and struggling to fulfil an airshow appearance programme, against crippling engine and airframe maintenance requirements. Owner Martin Caidin, a well-known aviator, writer, adventurer and member of the Confederate Air Force (CAF), had acquired the aircraft in January 1975,

appearing in it at many airshows around the US soon after. The aircraft, aptly registered N52JU, adorned with Luftwaffe markings and bearing the name *Iron Annie*, proved very popular with crowds and played a starring role in the CAF's spectacular airshow re-enactments of great World War Two air battles. Seen here at Opa Locka airport in Florida, in April 1983, the Junkers had gained some rather less than authentic markings by this time. *(Keith Gaskell)*

The contract between Lufthansa and Caidin required the aircraft to be delivered to Germany in satisfactory condition, in preparation for the airline's full restoration. Having spent so long in warm climates the Junkers lacked any kind of heating and de-icing facilities; however, delivery across the Atlantic was planned for December 1984. Terry Ritter, the flight engineer for the journey, commented at the time that this was the best time to fly: 'It's safer to fly in the depths of winter when it's too cold for ice to build up.' Well-known ferry pilot Clark

Woodward was contracted to command the Ju-52, assisted by co-pilot John Wilson. Routing up the US east coast, the Junkers plodded on at a sedate 100 knots, heading for Bangor, Maine. Engine problems in Maine delayed things slightly but Goose Bay, Newfoundland was eventually reached and the difficult transatlantic sector beckoned.

A further problem with the centre engine forced an emergency landing at Seven Islands, a small airport on the St Lawrence River, where it was discovered an engine

cylinder needed replacing. The route took the Ju-52 via Narsarsuaq, Greenland and Reykjavik, Iceland and, after more trouble from the centre engine forced its shutdown, the Junkers finally reached Prestwick on Scotland's west coast. The final leg of the epic journey to Hamburg, via Liverpool, saw a repeat of the engine problem but the aircraft finally touched down to cheering crowds after an amazing sixteen days and 4,970 miles.

Lufthansa deputy chairman Reinhardt Abraham, mindful of his airline's 60th anniversary in 1986, was looking for an apt way to celebrate this milestone. His aim was to acquire a Junkers Ju-52, the flagship of the airline's early years, when over two hundred examples were operated between 1932 and 1945, at the time the largest fleet of any one type in the world. The initial plan had been to restore the aircraft to its original condition. However, modern passenger-carrying safety requirements soon dictated that a complete rebuild was the only option. A very expensive option this would turn out to be, with much of the original skin needing replacement, which required the construction of a new extrusion machine to produce the corrugated metalwork. New wing spars were constructed, modern avionics installed and sixteen custom-made seats were fitted.

Authentic engine installation on any old aircraft places a compromise on the restoration, whether to install truly authentic originals or substitute with more-reliable and easily maintained alternatives. In the case of *Tante Ju*, its original BMW-132 engines were replaced by Caidin during its 1976 restoration with nine-cylinder Pratt & Whitney R-1340 S1 H1 Wasps, of 600 hp each. As the BMW-132 powerplants were licence-built Pratt & Whitney Hornet engines anyway, authenticity was retained.

Lufthansa's superbly restored Junkers has enjoyed an interesting career, which has seen operation in many countries. Delivered to the airline on 10 April 1936 as floatplane D-AQUI, it was leased soon afterwards to Norwegian operator Det Norske Luftfartselskap (DNL) where it took the markings LN-DAH, but was seized by the Germans in June 1940 and returned to Lufthansa as D-AQUI. After the war it re-entered passenger service in Norway, initially with the Norwegian Air Force, with serial 5489, but was later returned to DNL as LN-KAF in June 1945. In September 1947 a major rebuild was carried out, which involved replacing the entire fuselage and other major components taken from an ex-Luftwaffe example. However, with only 40 per cent of the original airframe now remaining, the aircraft was given the new manufacturer serial number of 130714, but retained the registration LN-KAF and

continued operation with SAS, the successor of DNL, until retirement in 1956. Shipped to Ecuador the following year, it was converted to land-plane configuration for Transportes Aéros Orientales SA, as HC-ABS, with which it operated until retirement in 1963. It remained inactive at Quito until American warbird collector and restorer Lester 'Bud' Weaver discovered the hulk in 1969, which had been left to rot. Re-registered N130LW, it was restored to basic airworthiness and ferried to Dixon, Illinois, where major wing corrosion was discovered which kept the Ju-52 grounded for a number of years. Sold at auction in August 1974, it became the property of Cannon Aircraft of Charlotte, North Carolina before being sold to Martin Caidin early the following year. Caidin obtained the appropriate registration marks N52JU and flew the Junkers to Tico airport in Florida, where it began a new and entertaining career on the US airshow circuit.

Unlike many other current airworthy Ju-52s, Lufthansa's aircraft is a genuine, German-built example, making its acquisition all the more special. Restoration was finally completed in April 1986 and it took flight again on the 6th of that month. To further the restoration, the airline applied to the German aviation authorities to have the original marks reallocated. However, as the modern-day German civilian registration sequence requires the second letter to denote the aircraft's weight category, this was impossible – the correct letter sequence for the Ju-52 would now be 'D-C...'. The Luftfahrtbundesampt (LBA), Germany's civil aviation licensing authority, eventually agreed to a one-time compromise which allowed the original markings to be painted prominently on the aircraft, with its official markings on the rear fuselage.

One of the last forces to operate the Junkers tri-motor design was the Spanish Air Force, which retired its final examples to the military base of Cuatro Vientos, near Madrid in the mid-1970s. Licence-built by Construcciones Aeronauticas SA (CASA), the ancient tri-motor transports represented an age and capability long-since overtaken by more-modern types and their replacement had been long overdue. It is from this source that many of the current airworthy examples were acquired, as the remaining aircraft were eagerly snapped up by various warbird collectors and museums.

Many were bought *en masse* by famed British collector Doug Arnold, who had them flown to the UK and stored at Blackbushe airport which, by the late 70s, resembled an airfield from the 1950s. With their Spanish markings crudely over-painted, the fleet slowly dwindled over the following years as, one by one, aircraft were sold and flown out to their new homes. These now range as far and wide as the National Air and Space Museum in Washington, D.C., Fantasy of Flight in Florida and the South African Historic Flight (SAHF).

This particular CASA 352-L, G-BFHG, the one-time T.2B-262, was acquired by Doug Arnold's Warbirds of Great Britain in November 1977. Delivered to Blackbushe, England, it remained inactive until purchased by Aces High in November 1984. In late 1992, Kermit Weeks acquired the CASA for inclusion in his ambitious and fast-expanding Fantasy of Flight attraction in Polk City, Florida, to which the airframe was transferred two years later, having been dismantled and shipped to Port Everglades.

The South African Airways Historic Flight (SAA HF), renamed the South African Historic Flight (SA HF), following restructuring at South African Airways, appears in a number of chapters of this book. Its successive achievements can all be traced back to a former Spanish Air Force CASA 352-L, obtained in 1980 to celebrate the 50th anniversary of the airline in 1984. This ambitious and very successful restoration became the cornerstone around which the highly respected and renowned SAA Historic Flight began. The aircraft had arrived in the UK in June 1978, one of the last of the type to be flown from Spain, having been damaged in storms at Cuatro Vientos in 1977, and required some work to render it airworthy again. Sold in 1980 to SAA, it was prepared for flight once again and departed Blackbushe in May 1981, bound for Bremen, West Germany, where the airframe was dismantled and shipped to South Africa.

SAA operated fifteen different Ju-52s before the outbreak of the World War Two, at which time eleven aircraft were incorporated into the Airways Wing of the South African Air Force. During this time the aircraft was modified to Pratt & Whitney power, with the installation of R-1340 radials, as used by the SAAF Harvards, thus allowing a plentiful supply of spares. The aircraft is painted to represent the airline's original aircraft, though it is registered in the 'vintage' category as ZS-UYU and operates under this call-sign. One of the major operating problems has proved to be the tyres, and even though a supply of originals was discovered in Germany a few years ago, their pre-war age has caused a few failures due to the lack of strength in the tyre walls. Nevertheless, the level of restoration lavished on the ageing airliner was a credit to the airline and helped establish the Historic Flight, providing a benchmark against which other restorations in the future would be judged. (*Martin E. Siegrist*)

The final examples of Ernst Zindel's simple, yet rugged, design to fly operationally in Europe were the trio of Ju-52s flown by the Swiss Air Force from its Dübendorf base. These extraordinary machines soldiered on until 1982, used mainly in the parachute-training role, having been operated continually by the air force since 1939. Following their retirement, two examples were acquired by the newly formed Vereinder Freunde des Museums der Schweizerischen (VFMS) – the Friends of the Museum of Swiss Airborne Troops, and funds were raised to maintain these unique aircraft in an operational capacity.

Now, some twenty years after their retirement from military service, Ju-Air, as their operator is now known, still maintains them in pristine condition. Founded in 1982, Ju-Air has a membership of over 160 volunteers and since its formation has flown almost 10,000 hours in the Ju-52s, carrying more than 170,000 passengers in that time.

Used for tours and excursions, as well as airshow appearances, the Ju-52s have been

seen in France, Germany and Austria as well as all over their native Switzerland. In addition, various promotional appointments have seen the aircraft flying to such disparate locations as Prague, Lanzarote in the Canary Islands and Egypt.

More than 5,000 examples of Junkers' workman-like Ju-52 were produced by the end of World War Two. A further 300-plus were manufactured under licence in Spain and France, known as the CASA 352-L and Amiot AAC.1 respectively, as late as the 1950s. The type saw service in the French Indo-Chinese conflict of 1949 and operated in the transport role for many air forces around the world.

The Ju-52's simple lines can be traced back to Dr Hugo Junkers' first designs for an all-metal monoplane, which went against the conventions of the time for biplane designs with wings mutually braced with struts and wires. Junkers maintained that an all-metal aircraft with an internal, cantilever wing structure would be stronger and safer. The Ju-52 was the culmination of a series of designs based on this principle, the corrugated metal skin of the wing and fuselage providing stiffening against torsion. The ingenious use of a full-span flap arrangement gave a double wing effect, and could be used to vary the camber and so increase the lift of the wing.

The Junkers Ju-52 was originally designed as a single-engined aircraft but, because of its simple lines and robust construction, development to a tri-motor was fairly straightforward. This improvement was introduced to increase the type's performance and improve the payload, and soon became standard, the type designation being amended to Ju-52/3m. Ju-Air's aircraft are all genuine Junkers-built examples, delivered to the Swiss Air Force in 1939. Originally conceived as a cargo carrier, the Ju-52's unobstructed cabin, at 21 feet long, could accommodate up to 10,600 lbs (4,800 kg) or up to nineteen passengers over a distance of 500 miles.

The Ju-52, with its basic features and unusual appearance of corrugated skin, was a vital link in the development of commercial air travel in the progressive pre-war era, when great advances were made at all levels of the industry, both in aircraft design and operation. Such advances were epitomised by the increasingly sophisticated designs of stressed-skin airliners, such as the Douglas DC-3.

The Ford Tri-motor was born of Henry Ford and his son Edsel's desire for a healthy commercial aircraft industry in the USA. In the mid-1920s commercial aviation in America was dominated by a number of foreign types, notably from the design offices of the Dutch manufacturer Fokker. The idea of increasing the performance of early, single-engined designs by the addition of two extra engines became popular, increasing reliability and performance at a stroke. Henry Ford had been so impressed by the performance of a single-engined, high-wing aircraft designed by William B. Stout, that he purchased five aircraft with which to start a freight service. When Stout reconfigured his design to tri-motor layout Ford bought out the Stout Metal Airplane Company and, thus, the original Ford-Stout 'Air Pullman' model, itself evolved from the German all-metal construction Junkers, became the famous 'Tin Goose'.

Scenic Airways was famous for operating the last examples of this famous airliner, using it on sightseeing tours of the Grand Canyon from the company's Las Vegas-McCarran International airport base. Superseded by more modern, comfortable and reliable de Havilland Canada Twin Otters, Scenic's surviving Tin Goose, N414H, was eventually retired and acquired by the Planes of Fame Air Museum. The immaculately maintained Tri-motor is kept in a fully airworthy condition and operates from the museum's Valle-Grand Canyon airport location.

Powered by three 600 hp Pratt & Whitney Wasp engines, the Tin Goose first flew on 11 June 1926 and could carry thirteen passengers at a cruising speed of 110 mph. By the end of production, in 1933, Ford had produced more than two hundred examples in five different variants, from the 3-AT to the 7-AT, having served over one hundred different operators including twenty-one examples purchased by the US Government for use by the army and navy as personnel transports. The Ford Tri-motor represented the cutting edge of air travel in its day, offering the fare-paying passenger of the time a giant leap forward in comfort and design.

Famed warbird owner Kermit Weeks has this pristine example of America's first 'true' airliner in his collection of veteran and vintage, types housed at his vast Fantasy of Flight aviation centre at Polk City, Florida. Tin Goose, N9651, a Model 5-AT of 1929 vintage which played a starring role in the Harrison Ford movie *Indiana Jones and the Temple of Doom*, was restored at Morgan Hills, California by previous owner, I. Perlitch, before being acquired by Weeks in 1992. This delightful view shows off the type's simple design and the very straightforward modifications required to convert the Ford from single to tri-motor. (*Gordon Bain*)

Another derivation of the Tin Goose was the SM-6000 Tri-motor, produced by the Stinson Aircraft Corporation. The type, which dates back to 1931, was originally produced with fabric-covered fuselage and wings but this was later replaced with a metal skin. Powered by three 215 hp Lycoming R-680 motors, the Stinson had a gross weight of 26,000 lb (11,800 kg), enabling carriage of up to ten passengers. Only two examples of this very rare antique survive to this day, and this award-winning and beautifully restored example, registered NC11153, finished in period American Airlines markings, is now owned and operated by prolific aircraft collector Greg Herrick, from his Anoka County airport base in Minneapolis.

It was last owned by Evergreen International, which had bought it at the Santa Monica Museum of Flying's Classic Aircraft and Memorabilia auction held in May 1990.

The Stinson remained grounded in Arizona for the next decade before being obtained by Herrick, to add to his already considerable fleet of similar vintage classic American types.

As air travel in the United States continued to grow in popularity Boeing was well placed to exploit this increased demand and, in 1930, introduced the Boeing Model 200 'Monomail'. This was the first all-metal stressed-skin monoplane designed for air transport which, despite its innovative design features, met with little success. It did, however, lay the groundwork for the twin-engined Model 247, an all-new aircraft designed to carry ten passengers, which would instantly relegate the slow and uncomfortable Fords and Fokkers to

secondary work. Boeing's new design featured levels of comfort seldom heard of in aircraft until then, with a heated and fully carpeted cabin, furnished with individual reclining passenger seats.

Of the seventy-six aircraft built, few still exist, of which only one is maintained in an airworthy condition. This pristine example is owned and operated by the Museum of Flight and was rebuilt over a number of years by Boeing employees at Paine Field, Everett. It was fully restored in period United Airlines livery, as N13347. The airline

operated sixty of the type and made history at the time with the unprecedented move of ordering the aircraft straight off the drawing board. This huge production order denied other operators the opportunity to purchase Boeing's new airliner, which, ironically, led United's competitor TWA, then known as Transcontinental and Western Airlines, to search for another type, the Douglas DC-2 – a move that would eventually spell the end for the Boeing 247. *(Gordon Reid)*

Hot on the heels of Boeing's brand-new and 'passenger-friendly' Model 247, the Douglas Aircraft Company was quick to re-enter the race for business from the airlines. United's huge order for sixty Boeing 247s had stifled further orders from other airlines but also laid down the gauntlet to other manufacturers to equal and even surpass the innovative features incorporated into the Boeing design. Douglas had already experienced the limelight with the DC-1, at the time the largest land-plane ever built. Its successor, the DC-2 would re-establish Douglas as a leader in the field of commercial air travel and provide the springboard for the revolutionary DC-3 design. TWA's urgent requirement for new equipment came about following governmental pressures to increase passenger safety. Douglas proposed a design capable of carrying twelve passengers, with a crew of two, over 1,000 miles at a speed of 150 mph. Such a specification offered significant advantages over Boeing's design and set in place the parameters for the DC-2.

The DC-2 survives in greater numbers than its rival the Boeing 247, with nine reported still extant. Flying examples of both types are rarer still. In 1982, the Douglas Historical Foundation was created by the Douglas Aircraft Company Management Club to oversee the restoration of this DC-2, which had been donated to the Donald Douglas Museum and Library in 1973 by its previous owner. Fourteen years after it last flew, the old Douglas took flight once again following major restorative work by Douglas employees and volunteers from the Historical Foundation. The aircraft is seen here in 1993 bearing the signature of its designer.

The DC-2 was to be an interim step between Donald Douglas's first foray into commercial air travel, the Douglas DC-1 of 1933, and the all-conquering DC-3, to which little introduction is needed. Its simplistic lines resembled the slightly smaller DC-1, but also represented a huge leap forward in design and performance. In upgrading the DC-1 design, the fuselage was lengthened to accommodate fourteen passengers, which required the repositioning of the wing to cater for an altered centre of gravity. With these changes and higher-power engines Douglas had, effectively, created a new aircraft, and so was born the DC-2.

NC1934D started life in March 1935. Built for Pan American as NC14271, it was transferred to the airline's South American subsidiary Panagra in October of that year. It was later sold to Avianca in Guatemala and eventually returned to the United States in 1953, when it was acquired by Johnson Flying Service of Missoula, Montana. Incorporated into the company's fleet as N4867V, the DC-2 was used for numerous duties, ranging from aerial retardant delivery dispensed through wing-mounted spray equipment, to parachute mount for Fire Service smoke-jumpers.

Douglas Historical Foundation's beautifully restored DC-2 took to the air again from Long Beach on 25 April 1987, a superb testimony to the skill and dedication of the Foundation's volunteer workforce. Initially restored in period TWA markings as a celebration of the first airline to operate the type, the aircraft spent a number of years being flown for display and commemorative duties, including a visit to TWA's base at St Louis in September 1994. However, persistent engine problems led to numerous groundings and also taxed the resources of the Donald Douglas Museum. Around this time the museum was purchased by the well-known warbird owner and businessman David Price, who then leased the DC-2 back to the Historical Foundation for a short while. The DC-2's problems continued and it was eventually grounded at Long Beach, in need of major

engine repairs. The DC-2 was eventually purchased by the Museum of Flight and transported to its Seattle headquarters, where it is currently under restoration once again.

The world's sole airworthy DC-2 captured aviation press headlines in 1999, when it undertook an epic transatlantic journey, on delivery to its new home, the Dutch National Aviation Museum Foundation, the Aviodome at Amsterdam Schiphol. This was the culmination of a lengthy and costly plan to return a vintage DC-2 to the Netherlands to create the centrepiece of a new exhibition celebrating 'Ninety Years of The Flying Dutchman'. The DC-2 is held in very high regard in the Netherlands, as winner of the handicapped section of the 1934 London to Melbourne MacRobertson air race. Operated by KLM, the aircraft completed the race with fare-paying passengers and flew over 1,000 miles more than the other entrants whilst operating an airline route, a feat which won the airline world-wide recognition.

Privately owned for many years by nuclear scientist Colgate Darden, this unique aircraft, based in south Mississippi, was seldom flown. It had masqueraded as the MacRobertson winner in 1983, when it was shipped to Europe to commemorate the 50th anniversary of the event. The aircraft was built in 1935 for the US Navy as Douglas R2D-1 Bureau Number 9993. Initially based at NAS Anacostia,

Washington D.C. it remained with the navy until being disposed of in August 1944. Sold as NC39165, it spent a short time flying commercially before being acquired by Darden. (*Paul van der Horst, via Paul van den Berg*)

Following a test flight on 13 July 1999, the delivery crew carried out intense flight training, the DC-2 eventually departing for Lexington, South Carolina nine days later to start an epic journey. Long-range auxiliary tanks were fitted, at the expense of a number of the luxurious seats, which were later replaced upon completion of the Atlantic crossing. The Netherlands Navy provided a P-3C Orion patrol aircraft as a 'shepherd' for the long overwater sector, which routed via Keflavik, eventually reaching the RAF base at Kinloss in northern Scotland on 4 August with nothing to report other than a deflated tail-wheel tyre on departure from Keflavik. Before reaching the Netherlands, the DC-2 staged via Bruntingthorpe for a final 'brush-up' in preparation for its triumphant arrival.

Escorted by two P-3Cs, an A-26 Invader and a Beech C-45, the DC-2 arrived overhead Amsterdam Schiphol on 14 August. Wearing authentic markings as worn by trophy winner PH-AJU, race number 44 emblazoned on the tail fin, the name *Uiver* (Stork) on the nose and KLM

Royal Dutch Airlines titles, the DC-2 had finally arrived. An extensive promotional tour was undertaken soon after. The aircraft will be maintained in full airworthy condition. (*Paul van der Horst, via Paul van den Berg*)

A Classic . . . by Any Other Name

Douglas DC-3 – Beautiful, bountiful, graceful, rugged, ubiquitous . . . quite simply, irreplaceable.

Widely recognised, not only by aviation enthusiasts, the DC-3 has probably touched more lives than any other aircraft in history. Its iconic status is recognised around the world where, more than sixty years since its first flight, it is still operating commercially. Hailed as a huge step forward in air transport at the time, the DC-3's success and longevity can be attributed to, amongst many factors, its simplicity of design and the perception and persistence of one man, Cyrus Rowlett Smith, of American Airlines. Circumstance and timing were also major influences on its success: its quality and superior performance set it apart from any competition. Such characteristics were soon recognised as the clouds of war loomed large, the military quickly embracing the benefits of the rugged design, which, as history would show, became the trademark of this unique aircraft.

This chapter is introduced by Dream Flight's immaculate C-47A, N101KC, seen close to its birthplace of Long Beach, California during 1998, from which it first took flight some fifty-five years earlier.

C-47-DL, N728G, beautifully restored and owned by Wiley Sanders, displays Douglas's famous and distinctive house colours, which represent the company's first-around-the-world triumph in April 1924. Originally, four Douglas World Cruiser aircraft left Santa Monica on 17 March to begin the epic journey, but two were lost in the attempt. A fifth aircraft later joined the survivors, which returned triumphantly 175 days later. This feat overwhelmed the American public and made headlines around the world, establishing beyond question the commitment of the Douglas Aircraft Company to aviation.

That the purposeful Douglas design was well suited to a wartime career is without question. The first 'true' military variant of the DC-3, designated the C-41 and destined to be the sole variant, was allocated the military serial 38-502 and delivered from Douglas's Santa Monica plant to the Army Air Corps in October 1938. Essentially a standard 'commercial' version of the DC-3

furnished with a VIP interior, it entered service at Bolling Field, Washington D.C., where it was operated by the First Staff Squadron transport and used by General H. H. 'Hap' Arnold, the Commander of the Air Corps.

After the war this unique 'Gooney' was loaned for a short time to Alaska Airlines as NC15473, before being transferred to the

CAA – Civil Aeronautics Authority (later FAA – Federal Aviation Administration) on 12 April 1948, where it took the registration NC12. Here it remained, giving sterling service until finally being withdrawn in 1977, having been re-registered N43 some years earlier.

Because of its significance, the airframe had originally been earmarked for preservation with the USAF Museum. However, it was transferred to Missouri State University as N54595. Commercial operation resumed again in 1985, with a number of different operators before the aircraft was acquired by the Otis Spunkmeyer Company, where it joined a number of similar types employed in the company's popular Sentimental Journeys operation, pleasure-flying in the San Francisco region.

In late 1993 the company decided to return the aircraft to its original Army Air Corps markings and apply for a more appropriate tail number. Allocated NC41HQ, the C-41 was beautifully restored by Aeroflair of Santa Maria, California which diligently returned this classic to its original splendour. In a supreme act of showmanship, Otis Spunkmeyer flew the C-41 to Europe in the summer of 1994 to commemorate the 50th anniversary of D-Day. The journey from California took nine gruelling days, the aircraft and crew enduring all manner of weather along the way before finally arriving in Edinburgh on the afternoon of 18 May. The visit was a great success, the C-41 taking part in the official flypast over Portsmouth harbour, on 5 June, in the presence of Her Majesty the Queen and President Clinton.

The genesis of the DC-3 goes back to American Airlines' President, C. R. Smith's proposals for an upgraded and improved version of the DC-2. The Douglas Sleeper Transport (DST) as it would be known, was originally conceived as a 'Super DC-2', offering improved comfort over its predecessor with better performance and a range capable of non-stop night-sleeper service between New York and Chicago. The result would be an almost completely new design, with little over 10 per cent commonality with the original DC-2, which was confirmed in an order from American Airlines, for ten DSTs, on 8 July 1935. The new design maintained the same basic layout, with increased wing and fin area, a longer and slightly recontoured fuselage and more-powerful engines. This order would be the foundation of America's burgeoning airline industry, as other airlines soon followed Smith's lead.

Next in the line of keen customers beating a path to Douglas's door was United Airlines, which was looking to augment its fleet of Boeing 247s, as the economics of the

DC-3 seemed to make far more sense. United's first aircraft, NC16070, was the subject of a stupendous restoration project in the late 1980s, by owner Larry Ray of Tucson, Arizona. A painstaking and lengthy renovation, over a period of years, eventually returned this classic craft to its former glory. Here, the DC-3 is seen looking forlorn at Tucson in early 1978, in the faded and peeling markings of Continental Airlines, its final commercial operator, prior to the aircraft's return to magnificence. (*Keith Gaskell*)

United Airlines' *Mainliner Reno* was part of a 1936 order covering ten Douglas DC-3A-197 'Skylounge' aircraft, an order which pioneered the soon-to-be very successful combination of DC-3 and Pratt & Whitney R-1830 Twin Wasp powerplant. The rationale behind this move was the requirement for more power, necessary for United's route network over the mountainous west coast region of America. Delivered to the airline in late November 1936, NC16070 helped expand United's coverage of the western United States until the type was phased out in October 1956. The fleet had flown some 400 million revenue miles and carried almost 13 million passengers during twenty years of sterling service.

Retired in 1953, with over 50,000 hours logged, N16070 was purchased by Leeward Aero Services and leased soon afterwards to Texas-based Pioneer Airlines which, in 1955, merged with Continental Airlines. The DC-3 soldiered on until finally being superseded by more-modern equipment in the mid-60s, at which point it was sold to the first of many small operators before being acquired by Tucson-based Hamilton Aviation in 1970. Hamilton ferried the DC-3 to its Arizona base, where it was then bought by Larry Ray for a reported $4,200 and entered a period of prolonged storage alongside the numerous other 'hulks' which abounded at the airport around this time. Early in 1986 Larry began a complete overhaul and refurbishment of the world's second-oldest DC-3, as seen here in May 1986. (*Keith Gaskell*)

The quality of work bestowed upon this valuable and significant DC-3 was second to none. The fuselage was polished to its original finish, with authentic United markings re-applied, the etching in the skin from these original marks still visible all those years later. Inside the cabin, Larry had the side and headlining fabric replaced and seating was installed. The aircraft's first post-restoration flight took place in December 1986, when it flew for the first time in sixteen years.

After restoration, N16070 led a very sedate existence with a few airshow appearances in the region before its owner moved the DC-3 from Tucson to Coolidge, some 80 miles north, where it kept company with a number of similar types employed in sky-diving work. By 1990, however, Larry had decided to give up on the delights of classic DC-3 ownership and entered his aircraft in the Santa Monica Museum of Flying's Classic Aircraft and Memorabilia auction, held in May of that year. Flown to Santa Monica, *Mainliner Reno* was the subject of much interest, with bidding finally being concluded successfully by Evergreen International Aviation, at

$165,000. After the auction the DC-3 was flown to Evergreen's Pinal Air Park base in Arizona, not far from where its journey to Santa Monica had begun. There it sat for the next seven years, part of Evergreen's vast collection of classic and antique aircraft. The owners finally had the DC-3 made airworthy again and ferried it to Fort Collins, Colorado in December 1997, where Darrell Skurich was contracted to prepare the aircraft for display at Evergreen's new air museum at McMinnville, Oregon.

Because of a shrewd clause in C. R. Smith's American Airlines contract with Douglas, the company was not allowed to sell any DSTs to other airlines until American's order had been fulfilled, thus guaranteeing American Airlines' lead over its rivals. United, the type's second customer, was quickly followed by TWA which was just as keen to acquire the new aircraft, which it named the 'Super Skyliner Sleeper'. TWA put its aircraft into service between New York and Los Angeles, a whole-day flight called the 'Sun Racer' service, which took from 8.30 am to 11.30 pm to reach its destination. Further routes were soon opened, with the passenger cabin changed

from an 8-sleeper berth / 9-sedan-chair arrangement to a more cost-effective 21-seat 'Super Skyliner' configuration.

Kansas City, Missouri-based Save-a-Connie (SAC), now known by its new name of the Airline History Museum, was keen to acquire an example of the DC-3 to restore and operate alongside the organisation's other examples of TWA's former classic airliners, the Lockheed Super Constellation and Martin 4-0-4. The museum's DC-3 is an early model, NC1945, which was built at Santa Monica in 1941, and flew with TWA between 1941 and 1952. It is one of the few surviving DC-3s with the original 24-passenger, 8-window arrangement, most

others being 21-passenger, 7-window configuration. After retirement from TWA it flew with North Central Airlines for fourteen years, and later with numerous charter and corporate operators, for a period which included a spell as an electronic test-bed based in California. Finally retired, it was flown to Roswell, New Mexico for storage, and eventual sale. Purchased by SAC in 1993, the DC-3 is currently undergoing a thorough restoration which should see it returned to the same outstanding condition as its stablemates. (*Foe Geldersma*)

The DC-3, in its many military guises as the C-47 to C-53, C-117 and R4D, served in almost every theatre of war. Five days after the Japanese attack on Pearl Harbor, President Theodore Roosevelt mobilised all civilian airliners into the Army Air Transport Command (ATC) and the Naval Air Transport Service (NATS). Existing airlines' DC-3s and those airframes still under construction were drafted into military service, the Government paying the airlines the going rate for their aircraft, with many aircraft flown by their commercial crews in military uniform, contracted to the ATC and NATS. The DC-3 had gone to war. In Europe, the Royal Air Force placed huge orders, through the British Purchasing Commission, for DC-3s to equip its many transport squadrons, which were later bolstered when the US Congress passed the Lend-Lease Act, which significantly increased the flow of much-needed airframes.

The Royal Air Force operates a C-47A as a memorial to the type and its dedicated aircrews, as part of the Battle of Britain Memorial Flight (BBMF) from its base at RAF Coningsby, Lincolnshire. The aircraft was delivered to Coningsby in 1993 wearing the markings of No. 271 Squadron, as Flight Lieutenant David Lord, DFC's aircraft, during the Arnhem campaign. The C-47A, or Dakota in RAF parlance, has since become both a popular airshow performer and an honoured participant in numerous commemorative events, as well as a being of immense value in training aircrew for the Flight's Avro Lancaster during the winter months when the bomber is inactive.

Built at Long Beach, this C-47 was delivered to the USAAF on 7 September 1943 as 42-24338, after which it was transferred to the Royal Canadian Air Force on 16 September, becoming Dakota Mk 3 serial number '661'. Having spent the war years and beyond in Canada, the Dakota eventually arrived in Europe in 1965, where it operated in support of the many RCAF fighter units assigned to NATO at that time. Declared surplus by the RCAF, '661' was acquired by Scottish Aviation Limited (SAL), on behalf of the Royal Aircraft Establishment (RAE), for use in sonar-buoy trials work off the west coast of Scotland, operating from the RAE base at West Freugh. Following refurbishment by SAL, the Dakota was delivered still wearing the markings '661', which were later changed to 'KG661' to comply with the UK military aircraft serial system. This was later discovered to be an error, these markings originally having been given to an airframe which crashed in 1944, and the new marks of ZA947 were allocated to correct this situation.

ZA947 continued in service with the RAE, later the Defence Research Agency (DRA), until 1992 when it was declared surplus to requirements. The Dakota was adopted by RAF Strike Command, and issued to BBMF in March 1993. It was flown to Coventry, where DC-3 specialists Air Atlantique carried out engineering and structural work, before being flown to RAF Marham for repainting. Delivered to its new home on 20 July 1993, it has since participated in numerous commemorations of wartime air transport campaigns, such as the 50th anniversaries of Operation *Overlord*, dropping parachutists at Pegasus Bridge, and Operation *Market Garden*, dropping paras onto Ginkel Heath, near Arnhem. These have been followed by numerous other forays into Europe for similar events. The aircraft also took part in the huge VE Day 50th anniversary flypast over London.

The renowned exploits of the DC-3 were also celebrated by Air Atlantique, the well-known operator of the classic 'Dak', as well as numerous other vintage types flown on *ad hoc* freight charter services throughout Europe. The airline operates a number of restored classic types as a form of flying museum, with certain types such as the DC-3 cleared for passenger pleasure flights. In the past the airline flew an example restored in period Northwest Airlines colours, and recently had one of its fleet painted to represent a Dakota of the Royal Air Force Transport Command. Repainted in early 1998 to coincide with the 50th anniversary celebrations of the Berlin Airlift, the Dakota wore its original British military serial alongside the civil registration and is fitted with a quick-change interior to permit fast reconfiguration from passenger- to freight-work.

The Dakota was built for the USAAF as C-47B, 44-76540, at the Douglas plant at Oklahoma City. It was diverted to the RAF as a Lend-Lease Dakota Mk IV, KN442, arriving in the UK on 24 March 1944, where it was assigned to No. 525 Squadron based at RAF Lyneham, Wiltshire. It went on to serve with No. 46 Squadron, and was eventually retired from military service in 1950 and sold to Starways in March 1952, taking the registration G-AMPZ. Its commercial service continued throughout the 1960s under various owners, including British United Airways and Silver City Airways, before a period of lease with the Pan American Indonesian Oil Co. Further lease work with Lebanese Air Transport saw the Dakota take up the marks OD-AEQ, before returning to the UK in 1965. A proposed sale to the Netherlands did not materialise, but during 1969 it did operate for a short while in Iceland as TF-IAV. Restored to G-AMPZ later that year, it resumed work with various UK operators, including Air Anglia (now part of KLM uk), Air Intra in Jersey as well as a brief spell in Ireland as EI-BDT, with Clyden Airways. Later still, it flew as an oil-dispersant sprayer with Harvest Air, under contract to the British Government, before becoming part of the Air Atlantique fleet, when the spraying contract was awarded to the latter company.

It could be claimed that events in history helped to make the DC-3 one of the world's most famous and mass-produced aircraft ever. However, even before the Gooney went to war it was carving out a reputation for itself in America's rapidly growing commercial airline industry. Over 400 DC-3s had been built by the time of America's entry into the war, with a further 149 orders still to fulfil. The immediate post-war years saw thousands of surplus DC-3s released by the military, enabling the resumption of commercial services interrupted by the war, as well as allowing hundreds of new, smaller operators to flourish. The US airline industry was quick to capitalise on the obvious benefits of cheap DC-3 airframes, and the type soon became the standard equipment of most airlines. Many companies began offering conversions from military airlifter to commercial transport. These 'local' modifications produced the hundreds of different airframe configurations now seen world-wide, with the result that very few surviving DC-3s are exactly the same. In recent years, the recognition of this history by many of the airlines which were founded, or achieved permanence, through the pioneering work of the DC-3 has led to many impressive restorations.

Northeast Airlines operated a small fleet of DC-3s on its US domestic network radiating from Massachusetts. N33623, a 1944 vintage example, has been beautifully restored by the Dakota Aviation Museum of Mason, New Hampshire to represent one of Northeast's early transports. Starting life as C-47A, 43-15749, the aircraft was sold as N36MK in 1954 to the Morrison Knudsen Company of Boise, Idaho, with which it operated until 1969 when it was sold to Pacific Inland Navigation Company. Soon afterwards it took up residency in Alaska, operating with numerous companies until it was sold in Canada in 1976, as C-GBYA. The Gooney migrated south during the mid-80s, and was registered to its current owners in September 1993. It is seen here attending the EAA (Experimental Aircraft Association)'s 'Sun 'n' Fun' fly-in at Lakeland-Linder airport in April 1995 alongside another superb restoration in the markings of Piedmont Airlines.

The legendary DC-3 is known the world over, by generations too young to understand the true impact the type had on the world of air transport. Many current DC-3 pilots were not even born when the type first flew, yet it continues to endure all manner of adversity in commercial operation.

The Carolina Historical Aviation Commission (CHAC) is yet another organisation that celebrates the Douglas DC-3. The Commission's fabulously turned-out example wears the colours of Piedmont Airlines, the North Carolina-based supplemental carrier which became part of US Air in August 1989. Piedmont Airlines became a DC-3 'operator' again following a proposal from the company's retired Chairman, Tom Davis, to restore one of its DC-3s for promotional purposes. It had been hoped that a Piedmont Airlines 'original' could be found but this was not to be, and the aircraft chosen was acquired from Basler Aviation at Oshkosh, well-known exponents of the type. The aircraft,

N44V, an early C-47A built at Long Beach as 41-38596, was flown for several years but, when corporate support was withdrawn by US Air in 1996, the airline was persuaded to sell the DC-3 to the CHAC. The organisation continues to operate the aircraft in its restored markings.

Simple yet functional, the Douglas DST/DC-3/C-47 series surpassed all records of aircraft production, with more than 10,650 examples produced between 1935 and 1947. Add to this figure anything between 2,000 and 8,000 more manufactured in the Soviet Union and Japan, and one can fully appreciate the impact Donald Douglas's world-beating design has had on aviation.

Beautifully restored by the Continental Airlines Historical Society is this 1940 vintage Santa Monica-produced Douglas DC-3, with the original starboard-side passenger-door configuration. The Society, a volunteer group made up of current and retired Continental Airlines staff, acquired the aircraft to help promote the heritage of the airline and its association with the DC-3, operating it for promotional projects and airshow work. Originally built for American Airlines as N25673 *Flagship Big Springs,* it served with the airline until its sale to Trans Texas Airlines in 1947. The Texan carrier was one of the many start-up companies formed in the post-war years, and continued to operate the DC-3 until the late 1960s, thanks to bountiful supplies of low-time engines acquired in the many

military aircraft surplus sales after the war. Sold to an aircraft brokerage company in 1969, the DC-3 was eventually purchased in 1975 by Provincetown Boston Airlines, taking the identity N130PB and later N30PB. It operated with the carrier until 1988, when the company became part of

Continental Airlines. Soon afterwards, a cash donation from Continental to the Historical Society began the long and painstaking process, culminating in one of the best DC-3 restorations to be seen.

The DC-3 is also well represented in Europe, in commercial operation with Air Atlantique in the UK as well as with numerous well-established preservation societies and organisations. A leader in this field has been the Stichting Dutch Dakota Association (DDA), formed in March 1982 with the purpose of purchasing, maintaining and operating historical aircraft, allowing its membership to enjoy the experience of flying in these ageing classics. The Association's first aircraft was acquired in April 1984, the former Finnish Air Force C-47A, DO-7, which was flown to DDA's base at Amsterdam-Schiphol following a major overhaul in Finland. The immaculately turned-out Dakota soon became a familiar sight at many European and UK airshows, carrying DDA members and sponsors and becoming part of the show in many cases. Its acquisition was well timed to coincide with the type's 50th anniversary celebrations, which were held in numerous locations in Europe in summer 1985.

Resplendent in period KLM 'Flying Dutchman' colours, the appropriately registered PH-DDA became the focus of many similar organisations throughout Europe involved with restoring and operating further examples of this

magnificent aircraft. The tragic loss of this historic aircraft and all aboard on 25 September 1996 was, therefore, met with dismay and stunned disbelief. The aircraft is seen here in happier times attending an airshow in the UK. (*Keith Gaskell*)

Three years after purchasing its first DC-3, the DDA acquired another example, originally with the intention of using it as a training aid for the upkeep of the original. This evolved into project 'Doornroosje' (Sleeping Beauty), the aim of which was to restore the aircraft fully and store it ready for flight in December 2010, on the occasion of the 75th anniversary of the type. As it turned out, the plan was abandoned by the DDA only four years later, after the organisation chose to return the DC-3 to airworthiness as soon as it was able. The extensive restoration programme, which saw the aircraft completely stripped down and reassembled over a period of twelve years, was finally completed in June 1999

and the immaculate Dakota took flight once again. Registered PH-DDZ, and magnificently finished in the colourful markings of Martin's Air Charter, the DC-3 has since joined the active DDA fleet and is flown occasionally from its Amsterdam base.

Sleeping Beauty started life as C-47A, 43-15288, rolling off the Long Beach production line in March 1944 to join the war effort. At the end of its military career, which remains a mystery due to the loss of its service records, the aircraft was retired to desert storage at Davis-Monthan AFB in Arizona, from where it was transferred to the FAA and earmarked for service with the Government of Somalia. Registered as

N161 by the FAA, the C-47 was eventually delivered to Somalia, in company with two other examples, and took the registration 6OS-AAA (later changed to 6O-SAA). It spent some time with the country's national airline before being re-registered N920 upon sale to new owner ATC Inc. of Reno, Nevada. The C-47 is thought to have remained in Africa at this time and to have been operated by Malta International Aviation Company, which specialised in DC-3 support, before being sold as SU-BFY to Pyramid Airlines in Egypt, in 1982, with whom it remained until 1985. The DDA eventually obtained the aircraft in February 1987 and ferried it to the Netherlands during May of that year. (*Michael Prophet*)

Nowhere is the passion for restoring the DC-3 more evident than in Europe, where the type is very well represented, with most countries having at least one airworthy example. Almost every European armed force operated the type and many national airlines were resurrected or established after the war using surplus military C-47s.

Airveteran OY is one such organisation, formed to restore and operate the classic transport and celebrate its association with Finnish aviation. Based at Helsinki airport, the group operates one of the most beautifully restored examples of the type, proudly finished in the colours of the national airline, Finnair. Throughout the vast number of variants and sub-types built, the classic lines of the Douglas DC-3 possess a simplistic style and grace which, even sixty years later, is still able to turn heads.

This view of Airveteran OY's DC-3, OH-LCH, clearly illustrates the level of dedication lavished on its refurbishment. The aircraft was one of seventeen airframes laid down at Douglas's Santa Monica plant for United Airlines, Northwest Airlines and Pan American World Airways, which were all requisitioned by the USAAF and pressed into service as C-53C Skytroopers. The C-53 models were essentially DC-3s built on military contract and intended as light troop-carriers and, consequently, were built without structural change from the DC-3. These seventeen examples, however, were finished as specialised troop-carriers and completed with the large port-side cargo door of the C-47.

This aircraft started life as NC34953, but entered service with the USAAF as serial number 43-2033, in December 1942. It flew in Europe with the 8th Air Force and was acquired by the Finnish Government after the war, for conversion to civilian airliner configuration and operation by Aero OY, better known as Finnish Airlines. Operating in this guise until 1960, it was

withdrawn for the next three years before being restored as a freighter. Sold in 1970 to the Finnish Air Force, it was allocated serial DO-11 and operated by the Air Force Transport Wing at Utti Air base. Airveteran

obtained the DC-3 in 1986, when it underwent a thorough restoration to its former glory, complete with a fully refurbished and very well-appointed passenger cabin.

Scandinavian Airlines System was a big post-war user of the DC-3 and, in recognition of this, Swedish group Flygande Veteraner was formed with the intention of restoring and operating a DC-3 to represent one of the many examples flown by the airline. The aircraft was built at Long Beach as C-47A, 43-30732, delivered to the USAAF on 5 October 1943 and assigned to the north African theatre. It later served with the 9th Air Force before being returned to the United States in September 1945. Released, along with many thousands of others, by the Reconstruction Finance Corporation, an American governmental agency set up to dispose of the vast stockpile of airframes declared surplus to requirements at the end of World War Two, the C-47 was sold to Canadair Aviation of Montreal, Canada in September 1946. Less than a year later it was registered as LN-IAF and sold to Det Norske Luftfartselskap AS in Oslo, Norway, from which it was transferred to SAS in August 1948 and, in keeping with the operator's tradition of naming its aircraft became *Fridtjof Viking*.

Leased to Linjeflyg of Sweden in 1957, it

took up the registration SE-CFP and three years later was acquired by the Swedish Air Force, where it took the markings 79006, operating with F7 Wing. Military service continued until 1983, at which point it was withdrawn and offered for disposal. Purchased the following year by the Flygande Veteraner association, the DC-3

was restored in its original SAS markings, complete with original fleet name and authentic polished-metal airframe. This grand old lady has since become a familiar sight at airshows and special events throughout Europe and is a fine testament to the commitment and enthusiasm of the group.

Another Nordic restoration, and yet another well worthy of praise for the level of restoration and devotion lavished upon it by its owners, is Dakota Norway's beautiful LN-WND, seen at the point of lift-off from Malmo-Sturup airport, Sweden in August 1997. This pristine example is operated from the small airfield of Sandefjord-Torp, near Oslo, for pleasure-flying and local tours by the society.

A Santa Monica-manufactured C-53D, 42-68823, it was accepted by the USAAF in June 1943 and delivered to Europe for operation by the 8th Air Force. Retired after the war, it was initially stored at the German airfield of Oberpfaffenhofen before being released to the Finnish Government and registered OH-LCG, for operation by Finnair. Sold in 1969 to the Finnish Air Force, it operated in a VIP role as DO-9 until finally retired in 1985, its duties taken over by the more modern Fokker Friendship. The Dakota was bought soon afterwards, along with a second example which was later resold, by a Norwegian

consortium with the intention of restoring the aircraft to airworthiness. Allocated the temporary registration of N59NA, the Dak obtained Norwegian certification in July 1986, becoming LN-WND.

One of the most prolific groups to have emerged in recent years in the world of classic airliner restoration and operation must surely be the South African Historic Flight. It has established itself as the foremost member of this exclusive fraternity and has built up an enviable reputation for first-class workmanship and professionalism in its unique operation of vintage airliners associated with the country's national airline. The group was set up by a number of current and former South African Airways personnel, with the intention of restoring and operating a Ju-52 for the airline's 50th anniversary celebrations. Since that time, however, the group has grown beyond all early expectations and become, without doubt, the leading light in the operation and restoration of classic propliners.

The Flight's DC-3 is ZS-BXF *Klapperkop*, a C-47A last operated by No. 44 Squadron, South African Air Force, as 6888. Delivered to the USAAF in November 1943 as 43-92320, it was soon allocated to the RAF and given the serial FZ572. Its record of wartime activities has been lost, but it is known that it served in the Middle East and was later acquired by the SAAF, which had

two squadrons operating in this region, becoming SAAF 6821 in January 1944. Taken over by South African Airways in 1948, it became ZS-BXF, and flew commercially for the next twenty-three years before returning to military service with the SAAF in 1971. Registered this time 6888, it flew in support of the military actions of the early 1970s in Angola and Namibia. One of two examples owned by the Flight, the DC-3, seen here in formation with the Flight's first DC-4, ZS-BMH, is kept busy, along with other fleet members, operating numerous holiday charters and special-event flights from its base at Swartkop. (*Martin E. Siegrist*)

Post-war, the DC-3 became the standard transport type for most airlines but other, more modern, designs were already in production and ready to relegate the DC-3 to second-line duties. New regulations in the USA called for higher standards of certification for these new types, thus relegating the DC-3 to secondary status in the airline world, denying it certification as a passenger aircraft. Strenuous protests by the airlines eventually overturned the proposal, although a number of options were considered by Douglas to address the situation of the time. One was to offer a modification to the standard DC-3 to improve its performance and operating economies, which would allow those airlines still using the DC-3 to compete with the new generation of airliners then emerging.

The 'Super DC-3', as it was called, consisted of a completely rebuilt fuselage incorporating a 39 inch fuselage 'plug' ahead of the wing, redesigned outer wing panels and an all-new vertical tail surface and increased-span horizontal tailplane. The new type was to be fitted with more-powerful engines, either Wright R-1820s or Pratt & Whitney R-2000 radials, both rated at 1,450 hp. The proposal was that airlines'

existing DC-3s could be upgraded for the 'modest' sum of between $140,000 and $200,000, depending upon the individual requirements of the airline. As history would eventually show, this ambitious plan was never fully embraced by the airlines, with only five aircraft completed, although the US Navy did recognise the potential and converted some of its airframes. In November 1985 the Lan-Dale Corporation of Tucson, Arizona

acquired former US Navy C-117D, Bu. No. 17116, with the intention of restoring it as the original Super DC-3. Their fine efforts produced this superbly finished restoration, wearing the classic Douglas registration, N30000 and finished in authentic house colours. Flown privately for a number of years from its Tucson base, the Super DC-3 was eventually sold in Mexico and operated as a commercial freighter.

Production of the DC-3 and all its variants ceased in 1946, with 10,651 produced in the USA and countless hundreds more in other countries. The unsuccessful commercial Super DC-3 project did eventually yield results, when the US Navy chose to upgrade 100 standard airframes to the new configuration, though even this was not enough to offset the enormous investment costs poured into the project by Douglas. The aircraft were converted from existing US Navy R4D-5; -6 and -7 airframes and given the new designation R4D-8 (later amended to C-117D in the July 1962 tri-service aircraft type standardisation programme). The navalised super DC-3s were fitted with uprated Wright R-1820-80 powerplants of 1,475 hp, and assigned brand-new Douglas construction serial numbers, in effect becoming new aircraft.

Even though the C-117D was the last of the C-47 line to operate with the US military, many examples still operating well into the late 1970s, the type is still far

less common in private ownership than its standard predecessor. One aircraft, however, has been returned to its glory

days and is regularly flown by its proud owner, Charles Clemments, of Miami, Florida.

Built at Oklahoma City under USAAF contract 03071-018 as a C-47B, and allocated USAAF serial 44-77035, the aircraft was delivered directly to the US Navy as an R4D-7 on 29 May 1952 as Bu. No. 99857. This aircraft was part of a batch of 3,378 C-47s which were allocated wrong manufacturer's serial numbers during construction, due to an error in the numbering system at the Douglas Long Beach and Oklahoma City plants, which went undetected until many aircraft had already left the factory. This was eventually corrected, but did give rise to the very

confusing situation of these airframes receiving dual identities, further compounded in this case, by the aircraft being one of the 100 US Navy airframes 'rebuilt' as an R4D-8/C-117D which were given new identities yet again. This confusion has meant exact build numbers and identities of many aircraft have never been fully established.

Charlie's acquisition of the Super Dak came about almost by accident. Originally in the market for a PBY Catalina, Charlie discovered a Stewart Davis Super Catalina conversion for sale by owner Jack Leavis, at

Opa Locka airport in southern Florida. Charlie was very interested in the PBY, but Leavis was keen to try and dispose of it along with a C-117D he also had for sale. During the negotiations, Leavis eventually offered the C-117D at a very keen price as part of the deal for the PBY. Realising this was probably too good to refuse, Charlie soon became the new owner of both and quickly realised that the Super Dak was actually much more practical than the PBY, and every bit as charismatic. Seen here at Opa Locka in October 1988, work had yet to begin on its long restoration.

Having restored both aircraft to airworthiness, Charlie ferried them to Fort Lauderdale International airport to begin their long and expensive refurbishment. The C-117D was in much better condition than the PBY but still required considerable work. With Charlie working out of his well-stocked tool truck on the ramp at Fort Lauderdale and aided by numerous close friends, work progressed slowly on the rebuild. Both engines were removed and thoroughly overhauled and the entire airframe inspected. Finally, the Super Dak was repainted to its former US Navy markings of Naval Air Station Midway, where it had operated as station hack before being retired from service in March 1977.

Fully restored to its former US Navy markings, the aircraft's registration was changed to the more appropriate N99857, and Charlie now enjoys the versatility the C-117 offers, revelling in its ability to haul friends and their luggage easily and in comfort. Its ample capacity is perfect for the necessary picnic furniture and drinks-coolers when attending airshows on long, hot weekends. During the 1995 EAA Sun 'n' Fun airshow, at Lakeland, Florida, the C-117 was used as the mount for the attending sky-diving team and is seen here departing for another drop.

Operated by the US Navy and Marines in many different roles from freight-hauler to VIP transport, the C-117D gave sterling service long after its predecessor, the C-47, was retired. The type served all over the world, ending its days as the standard mode of transport for the station flights of most bases. Evident in this view are the various airframe changes incorporated in the Super DC-3 modification programme, such as lengthened fuselage, increased tail area, fully enclosed main wheel units and modified wing-tips. Many of the original C-117D conversions survive, with almost every other airworthy example being flown on commercial freight work.

Charlie's aircraft, by comparison, is the only example privately owned and operated for pleasure still wearing its original military markings. Based at Tamiami airport in southern Florida, the aircraft is flown regularly, and in the wake of Hurricane Floyd, in summer 1999, Charlie donated the use of his aircraft to disaster relief work carried out by a local church, operating eighteen round-trip flights to Eleuthera in the Bahamas.

DC-4 Skymaster

Designed almost exclusively to satisfy a military requirement, the DC-4 would become the template for a very successful series of four-engined transports produced at Santa Monica.

No sooner had the DC-3 started to make its mark on the world than its designers were looking forward to a newer, bigger, design with twice its capacity and a range in excess of 2,200 miles. History shows that Douglas's first attempt at this met with failure; the design deemed to be too large and complex. It was not until 1939, following requests from American, Eastern and United Airlines, that Douglas once again looked at a new model, this time, however, much less ambitious. An unpressurised cabin, built to accommodate forty-two passengers, it would have a tricycle undercarriage. Power was originally

to be from four 1,000 hp Wright R-1820 engines, although in the event the design was finalised with Pratt & Whitney R-2000s of 1,450 hp. The new airliner was almost doomed once again, as war clouds gathered. Those aircraft already under construction were taken over by the Army Air Force, designated C-54 and pressed into service. With no prototype, the first C-54 flew in February 1942.

Manufactured in large numbers, both at Douglas's Santa Monica plant and a new, purpose-built factory in Chicago, over 1,000 of the type were eventually produced. The versatility of the new design ensured

its later success in the commercial world, many continuing in service well into the late 1960s and early 1970s. Today, the type is still utilised by many cargo operators and has been a favourite with many American air tanker operators flying the C-54 and DC-4 in the aerial fire-fighting role. One well-known operator is Aero Union which, in 1991, explored the potential of the C-54 as a warbird. C-54, N76AU was deconverted from fire-fighter configuration and repainted as an authentic war veteran and offered for sale.

Built as C-54D, 42-72442 and delivered to the USAAF in January 1945, the aircraft was immediately transferred to the RAF and given the serial KL977. Later, in 1946 it returned to US ownership when it was allocated the US Navy markings Bu. No. 91994 and served until retirement in July 1970, being sold to Aero Union four years later as N62296.

Wearing the nose art *Santa Monica Maid* and overall olive-drab camouflage the ex-fire bomber was offered for sale in 1991.

Fully overhauled and fitted with low-time engines the aircraft would have provided any capable operator with a show-stealing exhibit. Such plans were, perhaps, a little premature as private ownership and operation of such large and expensive aircraft as the C-54 was still rare. Sadly, the C-54 languished at Aero Union's Chico base, in northern California, donating many airframe parts and all its engines to others of the breed still employed in fighting fires. By early 2000 the C-54 had

been acquired by Aero Flite Inc., a Kingman, Arizona-based company that operates a number of similar types in the air tanker role. This spring-2001 view shows the aircraft in temporary storage at Kingman, with engines and control surfaces removed. Good fortune would shine again on the C-54, as Aero-Flite completed its restoration for re-entry into service in spring 2002 as Tanker 162.

Without doubt, the South African Historic Flight is the world's best-known operator of restored DC-4 aircraft. The Flight is part of the highly successful South African Airways Museum Society, formed to preserve South African Airways' unique aviation heritage. After the huge success of the Museum's Ju-52 restoration, there followed the ground-breaking introduction of DC-4, ZS-BMH into the fleet, a move only made possible after the type was withdrawn from military service with the SAAF in the early 1990s.

Acquired from the Air Force in March 1993, ZS-BMH is actually the last of the type to be built, having rolled off the production line in late July 1947, to enter service with SAA the following month. This last DC-4 was specifically requested by SAA to augment its existing fleet, and was manufactured at a time when Douglas had almost entirely moved over to production of the larger DC-6. As a result, it was almost hand-built, a quality to which its current crew can attest, due to its almost flawless flying qualities. This beautiful view shows the level of workmanship bestowed on the DC-4, resplendent in its original markings. (*Martin E. Siegrist*)

SAA's DC-4s were retired from commercial service in 1966, the majority moving to the SAAF, where No. 44 Squadron flew them from Waterkloof air base on general transport duties. As their Air Force service often took them into combat zones, the DC-4s soon received suitable combat colours and the bright, polished skin gave way to a drab-earth and dark-green camouflage pattern. Operating in support of UNITA in the Angolan War, these aircraft were often called upon to fly at almost treetop height, bringing them dangerously into the range of small-arms fire from the ground.

This view, taken at Waterkloof in February 1993, shows former SAAF 6908 alongside 6907, behind. The aircraft were becoming more difficult and expensive to operate and were finally retired in the early 1990s. A number of the ex-Air Force fleet would eventually find themselves back in the air once again, following in the wake of the South African Historic Flight's original restoration. (*Keith Gaskell*)

Although the official formation of the Historic Flight was not until 1 April 1994, its first commercial DC-4 flight was on 8 April 1993, when it took a party of passengers to the Zambezi Valley. Since its introduction into the Museum's fleet of active aircraft, DC-4, ZS-BMH has travelled far and wide, visiting Europe on a number of occasions. These have included participation in such celebrations as the 50th anniversary of the Berlin Airlift, the 50th anniversary of the opening of London-Heathrow airport as well as numerous airshow appearances during commercial Historic Flight visits from South Africa. The most ambitious excursion by the DC-4 was its visit to the EAA Airventure at Oshkosh, in July 1994. This epic journey began at Johannesburg on 19 July, routed via Luanda, Angola; Abidjan, Ivory Coast; Las Palmas; Lajes in the Azores; Gander, Newfoundland; Toronto and eventually Oshkosh on 27 July, where enthusiastic crowds greeted the DC-4's arrival. Such a momentous visit was also rewarded with an award for the Best Transport in the Classic category.

Like other DC-4s in the SAA fleet, named after a mountain range in South Africa, *Lebombo* became part of a fleet that

maintained a once-weekly link between Johannesburg and London. A journey of almost 6,500 miles, over an elapsed time of thirty-six hours with *en route* stops at Kisumu, Kenya, Khartoum and Malta, a far cry from today's non-stop jet services. During the early 1960s the DC-4s were ousted from their prestigious routes by faster and more comfortable Lockheed Constellations, relegating the DC-4s to secondary routes within South Africa, where they were reconfigured for higher-density seating, the plush forty-seat cabin giving way to a more functional sixty-seat layout.

Acquired back from the SAAF in March 1993, the DC-4 was flown to the Flight's then base at Jan Smuts airport, Johannesburg. Restoration work began soon afterwards by volunteers, mostly from SAA, which also provided hangar space and technical and engineering support. Flight crew for the DC-4, and most of the other aircraft in the fleet, were initially supplied by SAA, scheduled as part of its regular crew roster whenever possible. Support like this made such a historic operation much more manageable, but in 1998 new management at SAA brought about sweeping changes in the Flight's operations. Maintenance and hangar facilities were relinquished as the airline gave up its formal links with the Flight, which necessitated a move to the SAAF base of Swartkop, near Pretoria, the aircraft's last home when operated by No. 44 Squadron. Here, the sympathetic base commander was happy to allow the vintage airliners to share hangar and apron space with the Air Force's museum collection.

Following World War Two, the vast military fleets of C-54s were pensioned off and became very popular with many airlines. Such a surplus of cheap war transports did not help Douglas, which was keen to try and sell new civilian DC-4s incorporating all the improvements developed during the aircraft's wartime career. Large cancellations of orders for military C-54s already in production at the end of the war left Douglas with an abundance of partially built aircraft and,

although they were able to deliver brand-new aircraft to the airlines at short notice, few operators took them up. Ultimately, only seventy-nine aircraft were completed of the 235 airframes cancelled by the military, the final example being SAA's ZS-BMH, which was delivered to the airline on 9 August 1947.

Of the 150-plus DC-4s which survive today, most are flown as freighters and fire-bombers, their domain stretching from North America to deepest Africa, where

flying in support of famine relief has provided new work for many old and otherwise redundant transports. Not so with the South African Historic Flight which, in December 1995 supplanted its original aircraft with another of the breed, as the commercial operations of this ageing propliner continued to prove the economics of such a grand venture. Here, *Lebombo* is seen moments before touchdown at the end of yet another successful journey to the UK.

So successful had South African Historic Flight's DC-4 operations become that a second aircraft was acquired from the SAAF in 1995. The flight's chief pilot Flippie Vermeulen delivered the aircraft to Johannesburg on 16 December, ready for restoration work to begin the following summer. Originally delivered to SAA in May 1946 as ZS-AUB, *Outeniqua* served with the airline until retirement in August 1967 when, like the majority of SAA's DC-4 fleet, it was transferred to the Air Force.

Following a brief period of lease with Trek Airways soon after being released by SAA, the DC-4 served with No. 44 Squadron as 6905 until it was, once again, retired in the early 1990s.

The Air Force had maintained its DC-4s well but in order to reach the exacting standards required by the Historic Flight and the South African air transport authorities a major refurbishment programme was required. As this picture shows, this was achieved successfully, culminating in the aircraft's triumphant rollout in early 1997 wearing the period SAA colour scheme of polished-metal fuselage trimmed in blue, taking flight again on 15 March. However, these markings would only be temporary as the Historic Flight was to enter into a unique arrangement with a leading European airline that would see this DC-4 re-create airline history. (*Martin E. Siegrist*)

In September 1996, Swissair announced plans to celebrate fifty years of transatlantic air travel by the airline and also to operate a series of flights on an 'anniversary network' of routes throughout Europe as well as in Africa. The highlight of this venture was the ambitious proposal to lease a DC-4 from the South African Historic Flight to re-create the inaugural transatlantic crossing by a Swissair DC-4, on 2 May 1947. On this date DC-4, HB-ILI flew from Geneva bound for New York, with *en route* stops at Shannon and Gander.

So it was, on 21 March 1997, not long after having been rolled out in period SAA markings, ZS-AUB was repainted to represent Swissair's HB-ILI, in the airline's 1940s bare-metal scheme.

The DC-4 was flown briefly for filming and publicity purposes with representative Swiss marks before adopting the South African identity of ZU-ILI. It departed South Africa on 15 April following a period of crew-training by Swissair crews, bound for Zurich, where it arrived on 29 April. On a bright and sunny Friday 2 May the DC-4 departed Zurich bound for Geneva. Following much celebration and festivities, history was re-created when ZU-ILI took to the runway and made a text-book departure, climbing away with a full passenger-load of airline personnel and invited VIP guests, bound for their first refuelling stop in Ireland.

A two-night stop was made at Shannon before the flight resumed on 4 May and, once again, a fare-paying DC-4 passenger service set out on the long and arduous transatlantic crossing. The superb restoration by the SAHF ensured that passenger comforts on this long journey were paramount, as Swissair cabin attendants, in 1940s-style outfits, catered for the lucky passengers' every need. The DC-4 arrived in New York on 6 May, after another leisurely stopover in Gander, to be greeted by more celebration. (*Martin E. Siegrist*)

During the three-month-long lease period to Swissair, the DC-4 travelled extensively throughout Europe as well as its well-publicised forays across the Atlantic. The Swiss aviation authorities permitted the aircraft to fly as HB-ILI for a number of promotional flights, including a brief sortie over the Alps on 2 May, *en route* from Zurich to Geneva, in preparation for its commemorative 50th anniversary transatlantic flight later that day.

The South African Historic Flight's second DC-4 underwent a massive restoration programme in preparation for passenger operation. Like any of SAA's current fleet of modern-day airliners, the Historic Flight's aircraft are required to meet stringent standards. As such, the airframe was stripped back to its basic components and, as some of the airframe engineering records had been lost over the years, certain parts of the restoration were

treated as a worst-case scenario project and overhauled accordingly. Many spares for the aircraft were readily available in Africa, though certain items were obtained from other sources, notably North America. (*Martin E. Siegrist*)

During summer 1997, Swissair made much of the brief opportunity with its newest fleet member, and a second 'nostalgia' flight from Geneva to New York was undertaken in June. Following the same route as the first, the DC-4 completed the journey in 18 hours 30 minutes flying time, over a four-day period.

As the Flight's DC-4s were both received still wearing the drab camouflage of their previous operator, much hard work was needed to strip the paint and prepare them for their award-winning finish. As the majority of the finished scheme worn by ZS-AUB, and later when it masqueraded as Swissair's HB-ILI, consisted of polished bare metal, one can begin to understand the level of work involved in this task alone.

Following its three-month period of lease with Swissair, the DC-4 returned to South Africa and re-entered the Flight's hangar at Johannesburg airport for overhaul and application of yet another paint scheme. This time ZS-AUB emerged in a more contemporary South African Airways scheme, representative of that worn when the DC-4 bowed out of passenger operation in 1967. Since then, the aircraft has once again ventured north from its homeland, with a mammoth tour of Europe undertaken in 2000. The well-supported 'air safari' took in such places of interest as Zanzibar, Luxor in Egypt, and Malta before arriving in Basle-Mulhouse, having flown for more than thirty hours since leaving Lanseria. During its time in Europe, ZS-AUB made an appearance at the Royal International Air Tattoo at RAF Cottesmore in July that year, as well as attending Expo 2000, held at Hanover. (*Martin E. Siegrist*)

Opposite: The DC-4 purchase was the DDA's biggest undertaking and actually comprised two aircraft, former SAAF 6901 and 6906, the latter intended as a source of spares. SAAF 6901 was registered ZS-NUR in August 1995 and flown to Rand airport for routine maintenance before its sale to the DDA. Both Dutch-owned aircraft were subsequently flown to the SAA maintenance base at Johannesburg airport, where the DDA's president officially accepted the DC-4 on 3 November, following a test flight. The purchase of two aircraft enabled the best four engines to be fitted to ZS-NUR in preparation for its long delivery flight to Amsterdam-Schiphol, planned to arrive by mid-April in time to participate in the ILA show at Berlin, in company with the SAA HF's DC-4, ZS-BMH.

The DC-4's arrival at Schiphol was later rescheduled to 5 May, on which date the DC-4 made a ceremonial flypast over the city of Amsterdam, accompanied by the Association's DC-3, PH-DDA, before touching down right on time to an enthusiastic crowd of well-wishers. Resplendent in KLM's post-war 'Flying Dutchman' scheme, the aircraft still wore its temporary markings of ZS-NUR, required for crew-training and ferry purposes to the Netherlands, following which its allocated marks of PH-DDS (Dutch Dakota Skymaster) were applied.

Even before European enthusiasts of classic airliners enjoyed the sight and sound of restored African DC-4s in their skies, the Dutch Dakota Association had pioneered such an operation. This followed the Association's announcement on 22 September 1995 of its purchase of one of the best-preserved DC-4s in South Africa which, like those flown by the SA HF, came from among the former No. 44 Squadron SAAF examples stored at Swartkop air base after their retirement.

The former SAAF 6901 had previously operated with SAA as ZS-AUA, delivered in March 1946 as part of the final batch of DC-4s produced, and operated with SAA until its retirement in January 1966. It was subsequently transferred to the SAAF alongside most of the other former SAA DC-4s. Since its introduction into the DDA's extensive operation in May 1996, the DC-4 has become well known to those who regularly attend UK and European airshows, transporting DDA members to such events in the style of air travel of a bygone era.

From the simple premise of restoring and operating a veteran DC-3 in the Netherlands, the DDA had now grown into a well-respected and highly professional organisation, with a large fleet requiring much support. Apart from the obvious expense of flying and maintaining such a large aircraft for private use by the DDA membership, the aircraft presented no real obstacles in its operation. The simple and rugged airframe was well in keeping with Douglas's previous design, and had been well maintained by the SAAF. The powerful fourteen-cylinder Pratt & Whitney R-2000 Twin Wasp radials, which provide the DC-4 with a healthy cruise speed of 230 mph, presented no real problems for the DDA, particularly considering the healthy supply of spares acquired from the Air Force at the time of purchase.

The DC-4 did much to open up commercial air-travel in the immediate post-war years, when many national airlines began in earnest to re-establish their international air routes. In Europe KLM, Air France, SAS, SABENA and Swissair all started transatlantic services with the DC-4, whilst other operators such Pan American and Australian National Airways, flying on behalf of British Commonwealth Pacific Airlines, pioneered transpacific services. The DC-4 soon became a symbol of the resurgence of air travel and most US domestic operators were keen to catch up, taking advantage of the considerable surplus of former military C-54s available.

Such experiences of early, long-haul, passenger flying were now possible once again, the DDA helping to evoke memories of a far more genteel time, through its pioneering DC-3 and DC-4 operations. The simple pleasures of being much closer to the 'action' connected with early air-travel are easy to appreciate, compared to the more 'sanitised' way of air travel nowadays. The evocative smell of burned engine oil and AvGas, the cacophonous roar and belching blue smoke forever associated with engine-starts and the incessant rumblings and vibrations

throughout the passenger cabin: these are all experiences that should be enjoyed by everyone at least once, in order to understand and enjoy the great mystique that was air travel fifty years ago. Here,

DDA's beautiful DC-4 cruises at low level over the Dutch countryside, in a scene reminiscent of fifty years earlier. (*Michael S. Prophet*)

Opposite: After being accepted by the DDA at Johannesburg, the DC-4 underwent an extensive overhaul in the South African Historic Flight's hangar. Fully refurbished, with the cabin furnished with fifty business-class seats, the DC-4 was finally repainted in period KLM colours with the DDA logo and adorned with authentic 'De Fliegende Hollander' titles on the starboard cabin roof, repeated on the port side in English – 'The Flying Dutchman'.

Delivery to Holland began on the morning of 27 April 1996, under the command of DDA captains Anne Cor Groeneveld, Chris Peek and well-known Historic Flight DC-4 captain Flippie Vermeulen. The aircraft routed via Mombasa, carrying out a fly-by of the

Victoria Falls on the way, which were reached after almost ten hours' uneventful flying. After a two-day stop-over in Mombasa, the DC-4 was prepared for the longest single sector of its lengthy delivery flight, routing non-stop to Luxor, in Egypt. This flight took the aircraft over the Indian Ocean, tracking up the eastern coast of Africa, the DC-4 arriving in Egypt after eleven hours in the air without incident, a testimony to the quality of workmanship lavished on the aircraft in South Africa. Whilst at Luxor, the DC-4 was joined by former fleet-mate ZS-BMH, which had arrived from Djibouti, operating another South African Historic Flight 'air safari' tour, giving the Egyptian airport the unusual spectacle of two classics of

yesteryear parked amongst more-modern equipment. Departing Luxor the next morning, permission was granted for a fly-by of the Pyramids of Giza, near Cairo, before the Skymaster set course for Heraklion airport, in Crete, another four hours' flying time away. Here, another two-day stop-over was taken prior to setting out for the eight-hour leg to Antwerp, routing over the Mediterranean before making landfall over Italy, finally touching down in Belgium with nothing to report other than an unserviceable cabin heater. Finally, on the morning of 5 May the DC-4 arrived at its new home to begin a whole new chapter in its already long and distinguished career.

In the six years since the DDA began DC-4 operations, PH-DDS has travelled extensively throughout Europe. It has taken part in numerous special occasions, including the many commemorative events surrounding the 50th anniversary of the Berlin Airlift, during which the C-54 became a symbol of the supreme effort to liberate the beleaguered city. Given the obvious constraints on such a programme, both logistical and financial, the DC-4 proved to be extremely successful and ably demonstrated the ability of the DDA to carry off such an ambitious undertaking.

However, operation and maintenance of ageing aircraft, particularly for the carriage of passengers, places many burdens on an organisation. The DDA is bound to operate within the remit of the Joint Aviation Authorities' guidelines which stipulate that operation of ageing airliners must be in accordance with the EU's Joint Aviation Regulations (JAR). This requires that all maintenance work and procedures be carried out to the same standard and working practices as employed on modern-day passenger types. This, naturally, places a huge financial burden on the DDA, which

relies heavily upon a volunteer workforce and tight finances. Sadly, in late 2000 the DDA decided to suspend its DC-4 operations, preferring to concentrate on its core aircraft and *raison d'être*, the DC-3 Dakota. Consequently, PH-DDS flew its final operation from Schiphol on 5 November 2000 with a series of passenger pleasure-flights. The aircraft will be maintained by the DDA in a fully airworthy condition, but remain hangared awaiting possible sale. (*Paul van den Berg*)

The DDA's second DC-4, purchased at the same time as PH-DDS in September 1995, finally arrived at Schiphol on 4 June 1997. The aircraft, registered ZS-IPR and believed to be the second-oldest DC-4 still flying, has enjoyed an interesting and varied career. Originally built for the USAAF as a C-54A, serial 42-107469, it was acquired in December 1947 by Chicago and Southern Airways after demob from military service, and registered NC53103. Less than a year later it was sold to Philippine Airlines, becoming PI-C102, and flew for this carrier until it was sold to Thai Airways in July 1957, where it took up the markings HS-POE. Soon after, a return to military service with the Thai Air Force saw it revert to its original military marks until it was sold in 1967 to Botswana National Airways. Operating for various companies in Africa thereafter, the DC-4 was eventually taken on charge by the SAAF in 1981, where it took the markings 6906 with No. 44 Squadron.

Retired with the other SAAF examples, the DC-4 was acquired by the DDA in the same deal as its original aircraft, but remained in South Africa, offering airframe and engine parts for the original aircraft. Flown from Johannesburg by DDA captain Chris Peek, the aircraft was expected to remain hangared at Schiphol undergoing a complete 'D' check, which was expected to take up to three years to complete. It was intended to restore this airframe eventually to a similar standard to PH-DDS, but future plans for this veteran transport are still not confirmed. (*Michael S. Prophet*)

One image, above all others, typifies the truly amazing feat of the 1948 Allied airlift in support of the residents of the besieged city of West Berlin: that of a fully laden Douglas C-54 rumbling down the approach to Tempelhof, with yet another load of desperately needed supplies. The astounding feat of airmanship and co-ordinated effort by Great Britain, the United States and France in maintaining a lifeline for the city is now legendary. For the fledgling United States Air Force the Douglas C-54 Skymaster and its naval counterpart the R5D, born of another conflict, became the backbone of the airlift. Experienced pilots found themselves called back into uniform to fly food and coal. Over 300 Skymasters, capable of lifting a ten-ton load, proved to be reliable, dependable and forgiving cargo carriers. The unequalled operation that was the Berlin Airlift turned the tide against the Soviet blockade of the city and became one of the truly outstanding airborne humanitarian operations of all time.

In an effort to commemorate the 50th anniversary of the operation and also to provide a fitting tribute to those involved in the airlift, the Berlin Airlift Historical Foundation (BAHF) was formed in 1992 by Tim Chopp, a New Jersey-based corporate pilot. The main mission of the BAHF was to educate the public about the airlift as well as to preserve a C-54 in memory of the event that saved the city from collapse between June 1948 and May 1949. The Foundation's immaculately preserved C-54, N500EJ, is seen here over British coastal waters, during its well-publicised visit to Europe to commemorate the event, in 1998.

Tim Chopp began his search for a suitable aircraft with which to establish the BAHF in early 1992. The search would eventually lead to a meeting with Ed Johns, of Omni Aviation and Associates of Pontiac, Michigan, and owner of Douglas C-54R, N500EJ. The big Douglas had been one of the immaculately kept examples operated by Canadian freight operator Millardair from Toronto, before being acquired by Johns to fly automotive parts out of Pontiac on behalf of the various motor manufacturers in the region. Following the

closure of Johns' car-part operation, the C-54 had been stored at Toronto and was awaiting a buyer when Tim discovered it. Acquired on 22 December 1992, the C-54 was flown to the US Navy station at Lakehurst, New Jersey, where the Navy had generously donated hangar space to the Foundation so that restoration work could begin. The group later moved its maintenance base to Floyd Bennett Field, Brooklyn, New York, from which the C-54 now operates

Supported entirely by donations, the

BAHF began the task of restoring the ageing Skymaster, which culminated in its first public appearance at the McGuire AFB Open House in October 1994, still wearing its civilian colours but already adorned 'Spirit of Freedom'. Following this very important landmark achievement, the C-54 became the focal point of the organisation's efforts. During winter 1995 it was returned to its hangar for a full repaint, re-emerging soon afterwards in authentic 'Airlift' markings.

The ultimate goal of the BAHF was to fly the C-54 to Berlin in June 1998, to commemorate the monumental achievement. This aim was achieved, and given added poignancy by the equally significant journey to Europe of Vern Raburn's MATS Connie. Much preparation work was carried out in readiness for the historic crossing of the Atlantic: the C-54 underwent rigorous maintenance which saw all engine hoses and fuel lines replaced, a new, low-time engine fitted and the installation of long-range radios. Summer 1998 in the UK and Europe turned out to be a delight for all enthusiasts

of vintage propliners, as the airlift was re-enacted at dozens of different airshows. The MATS (Military Air Transport Service) C-121A made its first appearance at Woodford, near Manchester, in early June to perform alongside the C-54, which had arrived in Europe the previous month. The Woodford show afforded this unique and specially arranged formation sortie to announce the Connie's arrival, a sight unlikely to be repeated.

With its interior full of memorabilia and displays depicting the history of the siege of Berlin and its subsequent record-breaking airlift, the C-54 is a flying

museum. The aircraft had started life as C-54E allocated USAAF serial 44-9144, delivered on 30 May 1945, but was immediately transferred to the US Navy where it took the Bu. No. 90414. Converted to C-54R and transferred to the US Marine Corps, it was eventually retired in June 1973. Sold at auction two years later, it was then flown by a number of freight operators before being bought by Omni Aviation and Associates in September 1990, with which it continued its cargo hauling-until acquired by BAHF two years later.

Another project intended to commemorate the 50th anniversary of the Berlin Airlift, again involving the Douglas C-54, was not so successful, however. Central Air Services (CAS) owns a large fleet of Skymasters, which were employed mainly on fire-fighting and aerial-application contract work. Strangely, the aircraft chosen to depict an airlift veteran was the only true DC-4 in the fleet, all other fleet members being former military C-54s. This aircraft was built in 1946 for Northwest Airlines, with which it operated until being sold in 1961. Thereafter, its career progressed in a dubious manner as it came into the ownership of Hank Wharton, a notorious aviation character whose liaisons were sometimes less than legal. The aircraft was one of three that Wharton tried to register in Liberia, when attempting to start the airline Africa Air. The aircraft was given the marks EL-ADR in readiness but the venture failed, though Wharton would later acquire the aircraft himself, flying it on behalf of German carrier Lufthansa. The wandering DC-4 was sold in 1965 to Canadian operator Transair, registered CF-TAW, and was owned by two further US companies before being bought by Central Air Services in February 1976.

Registered N31356, and converted to an air tanker, number 117, it joined the handful of similar types operating throughout the western United States for CAS. In the mid-1990s this fleet eventually gathered at the Marana Regional airport at Avra Valley, Arizona, pending further contract work. At this time owner Jack Dempsay had the aircraft stripped to bare metal, revealing traces of its original Northwest scheme, and USAF-style markings applied using the manufacturer's serial number 42914 as identity. This May 1996 view shows the point at which the restoration ceased, and the aircraft remains in this condition.

Not far from Avra Valley's C-54 'graveyard', is another haven for old propliners and, until recently, home to another extensive fleet of C-54s. Biegert Aviation, based at Chandler Memorial airfield, south of Phoenix, is another operator synonymous with the C-54. Fourteen former US Navy aircraft were obtained in 1975 at military surplus sales and modified for aerial spraying duties. Although the majority of the fleet was withdrawn and parked-up by the early 1980s, a small number of aircraft were kept airworthy to operate lucrative freight charters on behalf of the US automotive industry, which often saw them taking off at short notice to destinations in Mexico.

Having a number of fully airworthy, yet often inactive, C-54s, Biegert Aviation was in a position to offer C-54/DC-4 aircrew training, and many pilots took the opportunity to add this historic type to their log books. Such work paid dividends and kept the aircraft gainfully employed between freight contracts as well as leading

to the sale of one airframe to a museum for full restoration. The remainder of Biegert's dormant, yet well-maintained, C-54s were eventually acquired by Alaskan air freight operators, who regarded these ageing workhorses as solid and reliable.

Returned to airworthiness by New Hampshire-based Atlantic Warbirds was Douglas C-54Q, N44914, a former Biegert Aviation bug-sprayer, seen here departing Geneseo, New York during the annual National Warplanes Museum's airshow in August 1996. The aircraft flew its last mission in 1979 when Biegert's spraying contract work came to an end and, with engines and airframe inhibited, the C-54 was parked alongside other similarly redundant types awaiting an uncertain future. Built for the USAAF as 44-72525, it immediately transferred to the US Navy as Bu. No. 56498, operating as such until retirement in April 1972.

Of the C-54s at Chandler in the early 1990s, Jim Vocell and Patrick Whitehouse, of Atlantic Warbirds, chose serial number 10630, alias N44914, as being the most suitable airframe available from which to begin their ambitious restoration project. The DC-4 looked in good shape and, with a grand total of 21,051 hours since rolling off the Santa Monica production line in March 1945, N44914 was the lowest-time airframe of the six Biegert had for sale. Work got under way soon after and, with most of the

airframe work completed, engine runs were carried out in September 1995. The sale to Atlantic Warbirds was completed in March 1996 and, following some crew-training at Chandler, the C-54 was delivered to its new home in New Hampshire. The C-54 was flown for a number of years in the attractive blue and yellow US Navy MATS 'Atlantic Division' scheme until lack of funds forced its grounding. (*Eric Quenardel*)

The Douglas Skymaster continues to lead a healthy life throughout the world, equally at home in the African bush ferrying passengers and general cargo or fire-fighting in the United States and Canada, where the type remains one of the most prolific and reliable aircraft operated in this demanding role. Continued and regular operation is the life-blood of such veteran transports as the C-54, whose ageing piston engines rely on regular use to help maintain their reliability. Standing alert for the US Forestry Service demands 100 per cent reliability from these more-than fifty-year-old veterans, which seldom fail to meet their call to action, thanks to the skill and dedication of their operators' maintenance teams. California-based Aero Union was probably the most prolific operator of the type in this role, though its once-teeming fleet is slowly being replaced by former Navy patrol bombers converted to air tankers, in the shape of the P-2 Neptune and P-3 Orion.

Dramatic departures, such as this from Ramona in southern California, are nothing unusual for the C-54, hauling another 2,000-gallon retardant load into the air with seeming ease.

Even though these classic airliners are now well over fifty years old, the careful maintenance and lavish attention they receive in order to sustain operations on America's fire-lines throughout the long, hot summer keep the airframes in top-class condition. With the increasing trend in the United States and throughout the world of restoring classic airliners and returning them to airworthiness, there remains great potential for more projects, thanks to the first-class upkeep of these ageing classic air-tankers by their various operators.

ARDCO (Aerial Retardant Delivery Company) operates out of Ryan Field, to the south-west of Tucson, Arizona, and has three beautifully maintained C-54s regularly employed on fire-fighting contracts throughout the south-west region of the USA. The sight and sound of a vintage airliner preparing to 'do battle' with a raging brush fire is quite unique and breathtaking. Here, ARDCO captain Steve Howland pulls C-54E N460WA around towards his attack line on a fire in the Ojai

region of southern California in October 1998. Formerly USAAF aircraft 44-9133, it was converted to air-tanker configuration in late 1975, having been retired from military service three years earlier.

The DC-4 was part of a fast-developing and long line of commercial transport successes by Douglas, creating the template for the hugely successful DC-6 and -7 range prior to the jet age. The type, hailed as a huge step forward in passenger air travel, was recognised by the world's leading airlines, and paved the way to massive advances in international air travel as the world recovered from the ravages of war. It is, therefore, a fitting tribute that so many examples of the Douglas Skymaster remain in regular operation the world over.

Veteran air-tanker captain Ted Mundell is at the controls of aerial fire-fighting specialist TBM's Tanker 65, C-54T, N8502R, as it climbs away from its regular contract assignment base at Ramona, to the north of San Diego, California. The aircraft still wears its former military scheme, from its latter days operating as the personal transport for the commander of United States Fleet Marine Force Atlantic, though high-visibility markings have been added to the wings and tail surfaces to aid identification in its current role.

Big Twins

The Curtis-Wright C-46 Commando, originally produced in 1936 as the CW-20, a 36-seat commercial transport intended for the airlines, was significantly bigger and heavier than the C-47 and was never a serious rival to the Douglas product. America's entry into World War Two changed the manufacturer's priorities, as the USAAF acquired airframes for use in the war effort. Redesignated C-46, the aircraft was the largest and heaviest twin-engined aircraft operated by the service and, whilst never as popular as its smaller Douglas rival, it did gain the huge respect and admiration of its crews as a 'can-do' type of aircraft. Over 3,000 were built, in four different variants, and served in all theatres of the war, though attrition was high and the type proved to be maintenance-intensive. Its greatest fame was earned from operating over the 'Hump' the demanding China – Burma – India theatre of operations, flying thousands of missions over the Himalayas following the closure of the land route by Japan.

The Commemorative Air Force, in the United States, operates two fully restored examples, including *Tinker Belle*, alias 44-78774 (N78774), which is flown by the CAF's Oklahoma Wing, operating from Oklahoma City.

The rugged C-46 Commando continued to serve the United States Air Force in Korea, where the type's immense carrying capacity and large freight doors were used to good effect, enabling the rapid unloading of much large-sized motorised equipment. Later still, the type was operated in small numbers by the Air Force's Special Air Warfare Center in the early years of the Vietnam War. The last serving military examples, flown by Air Force Reserve units, were withdrawn in 1960. Most were reduced to scrap, but a good number were sold onto the commercial market as freighters, many operating with some of the United States' leading cargo airlines.

The Commemorative Air Force's other Commando is the well-known and much-travelled *China Doll*, N53594, maintained and operated by the Southern California Wing, based at Camarillo airport, near Santa Barbara. The aircraft served for only five years with the military, initially operating from the Sedalia Army Air Station in Missouri. Following this it was transferred to Teterboro, New Jersey, before being sold as surplus to requirements in 1950. Operated variously as a freighter and pesticide sprayer, the airframe was eventually donated to the East Texas Wing

of the CAF. Christened *Humpty Dumpty*, its time in Texas was short-lived after a serious engine failure left the C-46 grounded and in need of expensive repairs. Members of the Southern California Wing rallied to raise the necessary $30,000 funds to acquire and install two new engines and the aircraft was eventually ferried to Van Nuys airport, in Los Angeles, in September 1981.

The C-46 is a huge beast, its towering bulk exaggerated by the 'double-bubble' fuselage. Powerful Pratt & Whitney R-2800 radials, rated at 2,000 hp, hauled the massive twin into the air giving an impressive payload potential of 15,000 lb, or up to fifty troops, over a 1,200 mile range at a cruising speed of 195 mph. These figures are part of the reason for its success in conveying essential supplies to the beleaguered forces in China and Burma during World War Two. The C-46 was flown by a crew of four, including a navigator and flight engineer, its flight deck made even more roomy in appearance by the large and low-set cabin windows, offering good views ahead and below, especially valuable when manoeuvring the massive twin on the ground.

China Doll is meticulously maintained by an enthusiastic team and is a regular participant on the United States airshow circuit, often spending weeks at a time away from its Californian base, on extended cross-country tours.

Curtis-Wright's large workhorse may not have enjoyed the same success as the Douglas twin, but did cultivate a successful career as a versatile freighter, being the chosen type for many operators in some of the most inhospitable regions throughout the world. Latterly, Central and South America have been the domain of this huge cargo-hauler, where air-freight is the only option available to many communities. The type is particularly popular in Bolivia and Colombia.

China Doll is operated as a flying museum, dedicated to the crews who flew and maintained this remarkable aircraft. Its incredible lifting capacity helped to maintain Air Transport Command's air delivery service over the Himalayas during World War Two, which, by July 1945, was achieving an incredible average of one aircraft every 1.3 minutes over the 'Hump'. So successful was this operation that the experience gained was used to great effect in setting up and operating the Berlin Airlift a few years later, in 1948.

When the Mid Atlantic Air Museum (MAAM)'s beautifully restored Martin 4-0-4, N450A made its first public appearance at the 1992 EAA Sun 'n' Fun fly-in at Lakeland, Florida, it heralded a new chapter in the restoration of classic airliners. In choosing to restore a Martin 4-0-4, the museum acknowledged the significance of commercial air travel from the more recent past, allowing this important, yet hitherto overlooked, avenue

of vintage aircraft restoration and operation to be recognised. The Martin broke new ground in the field of classic airliners, previously dominated by pre-war types and similar 'first generation' airliners, and represented the era when air travel became something to be enjoyed by everyone, and not just the wealthy or influential.

Beautifully restored in its original Eastern Airlines' famous and flamboyant 'Great Silver Fleet' markings, the MAAM's

Martin 4-0-4 is a vivid reminder of how air travel once was. Acquired by the museum in 1991, the airliner was one of only a handful of airworthy examples and one of the very few that still retained its full passenger interior. Based at Reading Regional airport in Pennsylvania, the Martin forms part of an important and growing collection of fully airworthy classic airliners currently under restoration and operated by MAAM.

MAAM's Martin began life in January 1952, delivered to Eastern Airlines, the largest operator of the type, and launch customer alongside TWA. Operated under the fleet name *Silver Falcon*, Eastern's 4-0-4s took over a vast amount of the airline's network, from Boston in the north to Miami in the south and inland as far as Chicago, Denver, Kansas City and Houston. The Martin 4-0-4s operated on many of the airline's internal routes during their ten years of service, the final examples lingering on until the end of 1962. In December 1962, taking the registration N149S, the museum's aircraft was sold to Southern Airways, where it was flown on routes linking many cities in Georgia, Alabama and Florida. Southern was the last major US airline to operate the 4-0-4, or any other large piston-engined type, when its final example was withdrawn in May 1978. N149S had been retired in 1972 at Atlanta and was sold three years later to the Twin City Travel Club in Minneapolis, Minnesota. The type's popularity with such operators did much to prolong their active lives after airline service ended. The Martin passed through the hands of numerous

other owners over the next few years, including Vero Monmouth Airlines until it was purchased by Vortex International in 1985, which operated the aircraft on executive charters until it was finally withdrawn in the late 1980s.

The aircraft languished at Miami International airport for a number of years, though its condition remained remarkably good, as seen here in October 1988. When it was purchased by the museum in summer 1991, a thorough inspection of the airframe was carried out and all necessary work to restore it to flying condition was completed in preparation for the ferry flight north to its new home. (*Keith Gaskell*)

Following its ground-breaking restoration of a Super Constellation in the late 1980s, Kansas City-based Save-a-Connie was keen to follow this unique achievement with something equally stunning and, of course, closely connected with the organisation's ancestral roots in TWA. Given the organisation's commitment to acquire significant propeller-driven commercial airliners from the period 1935 to 1960, a Martin 4-0-4 was a very desirable project.

SAC's Martin, N145S is a sister-ship to MAAM's aircraft and followed a very similar early life. Built for Eastern Airlines in January 1952, it was sold to Southern Airways in 1961, remaining with this operator until 1978 when it was sold to Dolphin Aviation. The Martin then spent the next few years flying for numerous operators in Florida on connector services for major carriers until it was stored in 1981. In 1985 it was acquired by Systems-International Airways though financial problems precluded full operation before the company folded. In September 1990 it was sold to SAC and eventually took flight, northbound to Kansas City three months later. (*Keith Gaskell*)

TWA's Martin 4-0-4s introduced the familiar and distinctive 'Brilliant White' scheme, which was to become the airline's trademark until the 'Twin Globe' scheme was introduced some years later. Although many Martins were later fitted with weather radar, none of TWA's examples were modified whilst with the airline and retained the blunt nose of the original design.

Martin 4-0-4 N145S had been discovered by the group in 1990, languishing on the ramp at Fort Lauderdale International airport in Florida, repossessed by a bank following the collapse of its last owner, a failed enterprise intending to use three Martins to transport gamblers and holidaymakers around the Caribbean. Following lengthy negotiations between SAC and the bank, title on the Martin was eventually transferred and Save-a-Connie took possession of the aircraft. Three long years of considerable toil by dedicated volunteers eventually paid off with yet

another stunning restoration by the group. SAC's Martin, seen here in formation with the Super Connie, is flown regularly, being a frequent participant at airshows throughout the Midwest region of the US. (*Foe Geldersma*)

On securing the deal for the Martin 4-0-4, Save-a-Connie also acquired the largest supply of spare Martin airframe parts in the world. This would prove to be a veritable 'gold-mine' when it was time to strip the airframe in preparation for its lengthy restoration. Unlike other airliners of similar vintage, the lower number of Martin 4-0-4s produced, together with the fewer examples still operational compared to the Convair 340/440 series, has resulted in a significantly reduced spare-parts supply. SAC carries out its own engine and airframe maintenance, as illustrated in this view of *Skyliner Kansas City* undergoing an engine change. Note the second Martin 4-0-4, N259S, in the background, which was owned by SAC for a short time in 1995 as a possible second restoration airframe.

Often confused with its close rival the Convair, the Martin 4-0-4 spent its entire lifespan in the shadow of this more successful contender for the US domestic airline market. The reasons for Martin's lack of success in this market can be attributed to numerous factors, though a number of serious accidents suffered by the earlier Martin 2-0-2 model may have unfairly given the 4-0-4 a tarnished image in the minds of the travelling public and airlines alike. Just as the earlier Martin

2-0-2 lost out to Convair's 240, through lack of cabin pressurisation and a smaller passenger cabin so, too, the Martin 4-0-4 with Convair's 340 and 440 models. Although the Martin was fully pressurised its useful passenger load, originally intended to be forty, was reduced by the airlines to thirty-six because of lack of cabin space, which, once again, put the type at a disadvantage against Convair. (*Foe Geldersma*)

When SAC purchased N145S, much thought was given to its future upkeep and plans were put in place to ensure a long and productive career, considering the time and effort expended in its restoration. The organisation began searching to acquire another airframe intended as a spares source to supplement its already considerable parts holding. The search eventually turned up a result, at the sleepy airfield of Bisbee-Douglas airport, in southern Arizona, close to the Mexican border. There, forlorn and abandoned behind some derelict wartime hangars, the group found the equally derelict Martin 4-0-4, N472M.

This particular example had, over the years, flown for Eastern, Ozark and Piedmont Airlines before joining Basler Flight Service for a period of four years. In August 1975 it was sold to Howard Coones, who had plans to create the ultimate crop sprayer. A number of other Martins had been modified for aerial application of granular pesticides but Coones's plans were for an elaborate, permanent system capable of dispersing liquid or dry material. This involved fabrication of a complicated plumbing system from two large tanks constructed inside the empty passenger cabin, the cost of which amounted to many times more than he had paid for the aircraft. Coones eventually operated three spray-equipped Martins, though by 1979 one had been destroyed during a spraying sortie and the remaining two were disposed of, N472M changing hands a number of times before it was eventually abandoned at Bisbee in 1980.

Another famous Martin operator is celebrated in yet another fantastic restoration of a 4-0-4, this time in the simple livery of Pacific Air Lines which, over a period of nine years, flew ten different examples. Operating from San Francisco, Pacific had flown DC-3s on its services throughout the western United States until the arrival of its first Martin 2-0-2s in 1952. The larger Martin 4-0-4 was introduced into the fleet in November 1959, with the arrival of the first of a number of former TWA aircraft. The airline received authority from the FAA to allow a higher-capacity seating configuration, with the granting of a Supplementary Type Certificate permitting an increase from forty to forty-four. Eventually, both the aircraft and the airline disappeared when, in 1967, Pacific operated its final Martin 4-0-4 passenger service before the airline was merged with Bonanza and West Coast Airlines the following year, to form Air West.

Martin 4-0-4, N636X, is proudly owned by Jeff Whitesell and operated from Camarillo airport in southern California, as the flagship of Airliners of America, an organisation set up by Jeff dedicated to the preservation, restoration and flying display of America's airline heritage. The Martin has become a very visual reminder of the organisation's aims and achievements, which include ambitious plans to build a world-class air museum with the history of airlines as its central theme. A regular on the west-coast airshow scene, the Martin is also available for luxury air-cruise excursions and charter work.

Jeff's association with the Martin 4-0-4 goes back a long way, indeed, this particular aircraft has a very special significance for him, having once been owned by his father, Bill Whitesell, and in his early flying career, Jeff often crewed the aircraft alongside his father and elder brother Bruce. The path that brought Jeff back in contact with his father's old aeroplane is an interesting one, which Jeff believes was meant to be. The aircraft was delivered to TWA in July 1952 as N40429, *Skyliner Paris*. Flown for seven years, it was then sold to California Airmotive Sales and reregistered N636 for operation by E. F. MacDonald Co., for which its passenger cabin was stripped and replaced with a luxurious sixteen-place corporate interior. Ownership changed again in 1965, re-registered as N636X for James McAllister Inc., the Martin continued its corporate lifestyle until April 1973, when Jeff's father acquired it.

Operating as Professional Air Transport, Bill Whitesell held a lucrative contract to fly the TV production team of *NFL Monday Night Football* around the country during the season. During the off-season the Martin was utilised by numerous

companies on special corporate packages and *ad hoc* charters to the Bahamas and Caribbean, its superb VIP interior being perfect for the role. FAA restrictions on such operations, coupled with the rocketing fuel prices of the early 1970s, eventually wound up the operation and the

Martin was sold at the end of 1975. A number of further owners then followed until the aircraft was finally withdrawn from use at Pueblo, Colorado in the late 1980s and offered for sale.

At this time Jeff was actively looking for a suitable DC-3 to restore and operate in the colours of Western Airlines, with which he had started his commercial airline career. Acutely aware that many of America's pioneering airlines had been consigned to history, either through bankruptcy or mergers, Jeff had long held a desire to establish a living museum dedicated to the staff and crews of the many airlines which were now but a distant memory. His search took him to an auction in Billings, Montana, though the DC-3 and DC-4 on offer both proved too much for his meagre budget. Not long afterwards, however, a tip from a fellow sentimentalist sent Jeff to look at a Martin 4-0-4 parked in the weeds at Pueblo, Colorado which, according to local rumour, had been one of a number of 4-0-4s converted for VIP use. Although outside storage had left the airframe a little weathered, close inspection revealed it was none other than N636X, Jeff's father's old aircraft, and upon entering the cabin the original sixteen-seat VIP interior was found to be still in place, exactly as it had been all those years ago.

A deal was finally concluded in June 1994 to purchase the Martin and, following six weeks on-site renovation, the aircraft was flown to Seattle where a joint project to fully restore the aircraft was set up with the South Seattle Community College. A rather apt scheme was chosen for the restored

Martin; being based on the west coast, the colours of Pacific Airlines seemed quite appropriate. The Martin is still fitted with the original engines as when Jeff worked on it over twenty years ago and, with only 22,000 hours in the log book, is the lowest-time Martin 4-0-4 still flying. (*Jeff Whitesell*)

Of the 103 Martin 4-0-4s built, Eastern Airlines and TWA purchased all but two and, but for the type's problematic reputation, unfairly inherited from its predecessor, the whole Martin 4-0-4 story could have been so different. The Glenn L. Martin Company had designed the Model 4-0-4 to be the first production airliner stressed for conversion to turbine power, expecting these latest-technology powerplants to be released by the military for commercial use within three to five years. The extended gestation of the turbine engine into something of value to the commercial world eventually closed off this potentially lucrative avenue for Martin as, by the time Allison had perfected its 501 turbo-prop, the Martin was long out of production. The final nail in the Martin 4-0-4's coffin was its failure to secure the Air Force's contract for the T-29 advanced bombardier trainer, awarded to Convair. Had Martin won this pivotal contract, which sustained production of over 500

extra airframes, then it could be speculated that the company might have eclipsed Convair and the type could have taken an altogether different path. As it was, by 1953,

Martin had suffered reported losses of over $45 million and, quite wisely, decided to abandon all further commercial aircraft production.

The Martin 4-0-4 can be regarded as one of the more successful corporate developments of any modern airliner prior to the lavish conversions of many jet airliners of today. Many of America's top entertainment artists and sportsmen chose the Martin as their preferred mode of transport with names such as Frank Sinatra, Ray Charles, The Nashville Brass and The Doobie Brothers band all enjoying the type's reliability and

comfort. Martin 4-0-4s would continue in this corporate niche market, serving as executive transport for numerous property development companies and travel clubs throughout the 1960s and 70s. One example was also flown for the US Atomic Energy Commission where it was modified to incorporate an infra-red scanner and air sampling equipment.

Although wearing Pacific Air Lines'

simple yet smart scheme, this particular aircraft is actually something rather special. It is furnished with a plush sixteen-seat interior, complete with a fourteen-carat gold-leaf flight-deck instrument panel, Colombian-leather-trimmed control wheels, and luxuriously appointed bathroom furnishings. Jeff Whitesell can be rightly proud of his very personal mount.

Martin 4-0-4, N636X now operates from Jeff's local airport, Camarillo, in Ventura County, north of Los Angeles, alongside a number of other rather well-known propliners. The Martin flies most weekends during the summer and has become a regular participant in the region's airshow circuit, as well as being a popular attraction for corporate or special-events charters, where its palatial interior sets it apart from the norm. Regular sunset charters are also part of the Airliners of America portfolio, during which the lucky passengers can enjoy a scenic view of the Channel islands off the southern California coast, whilst sampling a champagne dinner in the Martin's unique and spacious cabin.

Naturally enthusiastic about his unique aircraft, Jeff is keen to use the Martin to further his Airliners of America project. In this view, the open cabin window of George Hulett's Twin Bonanza frames the subject well on its return to Camarillo at the end of the photo-shoot specially arranged for this book.

As described, the Martin 4-0-4 gained a very good reputation and an enthusiastic following as a corporate and executive transport throughout its mid-to-later life. As its time with the front-line carriers was drawing to a close it seemed that almost as many examples were being acquired by corporations and celebrities, as second-tier operators. Slowly, as bizjets came to the fore, the Martin's celebrity lifestyle began to wane, although one particular rock group maintained a connection with the ageing propliner until the early 1980s. The Doobie Brothers used four different Martin 4-0-4s from the mid-1970s through to the early 80s, their plush executive cabins giving rise to the name 'Doobie Liners'. The aircraft wore simple markings with the group's distinctive emblem on the tail.

By the mid-1980s, the three surviving 'Doobie Liners' had been withdrawn, one was sold for airframe instructional training at Miami and the others were parked-up at Chino, California, still owned by Sam Stewart, who had operated them on behalf of the group. Of these, one was eventually dismantled and now resides in a San Francisco restaurant, but Stewart harboured a desire to return his last Martin to flight status. In this view, taken at Chino in April 1980, N3711K is seen alongside its sister-ship, N467M, awaiting an uncertain future. (*Keith Gaskell*)

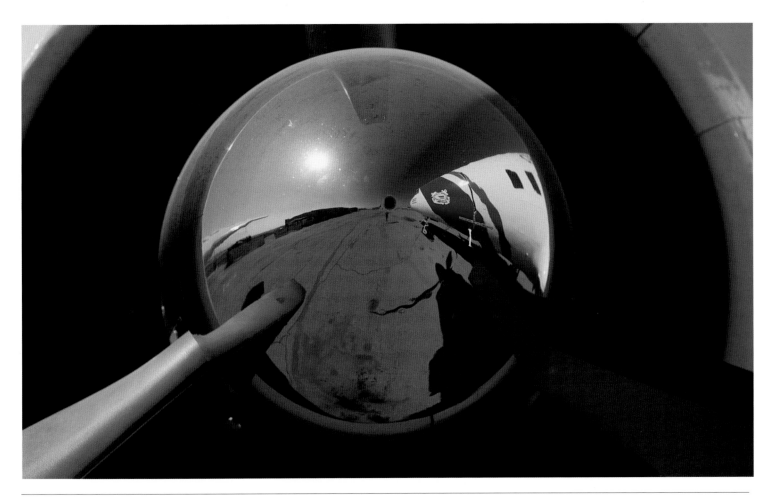

Martin 4-0-4, N3711K began life as Eastern Airlines' N487A, delivered to the airline on 13 November 1952. It served for almost exactly ten years until its sale to Charlotte Aircraft Corp. in December 1962, from which it was leased to Aerojet-General Corp. for a short time. Its corporate duties then continued with, firstly, Kimbell Milling Company in January 1964, where it was allocated the new marks of N3711K and, later, the Huber Investment Corp., whose Huber Homes division used the aircraft to transport prospective property investors around its various locations. In October 1978 it was bought by Sam Stewart, doing business as Monarch Airlines, and operated by Stewart as personal transport around the USA and Canada for a number of famous musical acts, including The Beach Boys, Foreigner, Lionel Ritchie and, of course, The Doobie Brothers. For most of its corporate life this Martin was fitted with large propeller spinners, giving the aircraft an unusually distinctive look.

In 1996, following many years of inactivity at Chino, Stewart ferried his aircraft a short distance to the small airfield of Rialto, California where a transformation would begin, to restore the aircraft to an award-winning standard, complete with a very distinctive colour scheme. In October 1998 Stewart re-registered the Martin as N404CG, appropriate marks to complete its restoration and transformation into one of the two US Coast Guard examples flown by the service between 1952 and 1969.

The superb restoration job was very much a Stewart family affair, with Sam assisted by his wife Donna, sons Ted, Neil and Brett as well as various family friends from the aviation community and Claire Aviation at Rialto. Started in 1997, the whole job took almost two years to complete and cost more than $250,000. The award-winning airframe restoration was complemented by an equally stunning interior completed by EB Custom Interiors, which was responsible for the cabin refurbishment, which authentically represents that of the Coast Guard's aircraft. Painted to represent a Martin VC-3A, as the type was known in Coast Guard service, it wears full livery and base assignment titles of Arlington, on the nose. The spinners were stripped and buffed to a highly polished finish and, whilst not fully authentic with a Coast Guard aircraft, help to provide the finishing touch to an outstanding and unique restoration.

The Martin restoration was completed in autumn 1998 and the following year made its first appearance at the annual EAA Sun 'n' Fun event at Lakeland, Florida, where it was the Judges' Choice in the Heavy Transport category. Later that year, at the EAA Airventure show at Oshkosh, the aircraft once again collected honours, this time being awarded first place as Best Transport aircraft at the show. Since then it has attended numerous airshows throughout the United States and spends its winters in the familiar surroundings of Chino in California. The US Coast Guard was the only original military customer of the Martin 4-0-4, and the only other customer of new airframes apart from Eastern Airlines and TWA. The original VC-3A 1282 operated for a short time with the US Navy, after retirement from USCG service, in a similar role to that at the Coast Guard, of VIP transport, with Naval Air Reserve Training Unit VR-52, until the aircraft's retirement in 1970. The aircraft was then donated to an aviation training school which later sold it to a charter operator, in whose service it was destroyed in a crash in Venezuela in November 1978.

Even though Martin 4-0-4 production never reached the numbers expected, the type has survived remarkably well. Although one or two reportedly still operate in South America, the type is no longer in service in the US, whilst its close rivals the Convair 340 and 440 continue in freight and air cargo operations. It is ironic to consider that the life expectancy of the Convair series has been considerably extended through its conversion to turbine power whilst the Martin, originally conceived with the aim of using turbine power, never actually accomplished this. However, at the twilight of its career the Martin 4-0-4 did achieve distinction in a role quite far-removed from that envisaged in 1950, that of aerial application, or crop sprayer. The type's docile flying characteristics made it suitable for this kind of operation, though at least three aircraft were lost through accidents. A number of former 'ag planes' still exist, including two airframes converted by Clayton Curtis which, together with N461M, shown here, are stored at Sheridan County Airport, Wyoming. This former Ozark Airlines aircraft was acquired by Curtis as a spares source and was never actually converted.

Perhaps Convair's single most important contract for the 340/440 series was from the United States Air Force. The Air Force had already chosen the smaller 240 for its multipurpose T-29 navigation/bombardier/aero-medical transport and multi-engine crew trainer and transport variant, the C-131A. Once again, the Air Force turned to Convair to satisfy its requirement for a medium-sized passenger- and freight-carrier, based upon the commercial model 340/440 series. Four separate contracts were issued for a total of eighty-six airframes, delivered as the C-131B equipped for freight and cargo duties, with a large rear side-cargo door and strengthened floor, and the C-131D model, which was basically the commercial Model 440 and utilised in the staff transport role.

This interesting comparison of first- and second-generation USAF transports was shot in April 2000 at the annual EAA Sun 'n' Fun airshow, which is held at Lakeland, Florida, every spring. The Berlin Airlift Historical Foundation's C-54 is framed below the nose of Classic Wings' unique C-131D, 54-2809, so far the only fully restored, privately owned and operated example of the type.

The USAF's first C-131s, the 'A' model based upon the Convair 240, were originally delivered to the Military Air Transport Service in 1954. Subsequently, the larger, and more numerous C-131B and D variants served most commands in the service, from Air Force Logistics to Air Defense Command. Many of the early 'B' models were variously operated as test-beds by Air Research and Development Command and Air Force Systems Command, operating with numerous modifications and often fitted with one or two T-41 gas-turbine units, pod-mounted under the wing centre-section.

Latterly, the C-131Bs and Ds in the Air Force became the preferred support aircraft for most Air National Guard units, where the type's range and payload were more than adequate for most ANG squadrons' requirements. Indeed, the C-131D was the last large, piston-engined aircraft type operated by the USAF, this chapter in Air Force history finally having ended in February 1988. Classic Wings' Convair is seen here in October 1996, in a Tucson salvage yard, having been disposed of by the military and sold to a Mexican freight operator. The aircraft had been acquired as a source of spares for other operational

examples, though more specifically for its two valuable, low-timed, Pratt & Whitney R-2800 radial engines. Following engine removal, the otherwise complete airframe remained parked in various surplus yards around the Davis-Monthan perimeter, still in remarkably good shape, with little more than 20,000 hours in the log. The future seemed uncertain for this aircraft as, being a 'D' model based on the passenger Convairliner, it lacked the cargo configuration of the 'B' model, making it of little value commercially.

During 1996, father and son Barry and Scott Holm, from Vero Beach, Florida, had been looking to acquire a suitable aircraft in the warbird category. Originally, their ideas were focused on a Douglas A-26 Invader. However, lack of suitable airframes soon terminated that line of enquiry and thoughts turned to something different. The Convair offered everything Barry and Scott required, a solid military history, an affordable purchase price and an airframe large enough to be utilised for public walk-through at air displays, where the type's extensive military career could be re-created and shown through various displays in the passenger cabin. On discovering the C-131, plans were soon drawn up for its purchase and Classic Wings Inc. was formed as the operating group for this ambitious project.

Western International Aviation Inc. was contracted to carry out a thorough inspection of the airframe and, subsequently, the restoration. The aircraft was moved into its extensive facility adjacent to Davis-Monthan in mid-1997 and the restoration began. The airframe was found to be in quite good condition, though a few areas of major corrosion were discovered which required the replacement of the horizontal stabiliser and panels on the wing trailing-edge. Two new QEC (Quick Engine Change) assemblies were needed, together with replacement power units. One engine was obtained from a surplus C-123 Provider, which used a slightly different version of the R-2800, the -99W. This required a new engine-accessory package to bring it up to the same specification as the Convair's original -103W engine, fitted with a supercharger, required to run the cabin-pressurisation system on the aircraft, this being the only C-131 in the USA flying with an operational pressurisation system.

During its thirteen-month restoration, the Convair was returned to an almost factory-fresh condition. The flight deck was completely stripped and rebuilt, with fully overhauled flight instruments fitted into the newly refurbished panels. The crew seats were completely reupholstered, giving the flight deck the look of a brand-new aircraft.

Restoration was finally completed in November 1997 and appropriately registered N131CW, the C-131 took flight again the same month, the first time it had flown in eleven years, and was delivered to Classic Wings in Florida soon afterwards.

Classic Wings' C-131D made its show debut at the 1998 Valiant Air Command show at Tico airport in March. It was also the largest aircraft on show at the EAA Sun 'n' Fun fly-in at Lakeland the following month, as seen here, where its arrival was greeted with applause from the gathered crowd. The restoration by Western International earned the aircraft an award at the prestigious EAA Airventure at Oshkosh later the same year. This success will no doubt spur the recognition of other, less-celebrated types which richly deserve to be restored.

C-131D, 54-2809 was manufactured at Convair's San Diego, California plant in July 1954, as a Model 340-67, and was allocated the test registration N8426H for its first flight. Delivered to the Air Force on 26 October, it took up its first assignment with the 1299th Air Transport Squadron at Bolling AFB soon afterwards. The aircraft was then shuttled around between numerous similar units for the next decade before being reassigned to the 2nd Air Delivery Group at Hamilton AFB until it was withdrawn from service in June 1975 and flown to the military 'boneyard' at Davis-Monthan AFB. Brought out of storage a mere ten months later, it was then dispatched to the Maryland Air National Guard where it became the unit hack for the 135th Tactical Airlift Group at the Glenn L. Martin State Airport in Baltimore. Its final assignment was with the 102nd Tactical Fighter Group, at Otis Air National Guard Base in Massachusetts, in May 1979. Here it was adorned with the unit's stylish two-tone blue 'Cape Cod' markings on its cabin roof, as it went about its daily duties supporting the unit's F-106 Delta Darts and, later, F-15 Eagles. Final retirement from military service came on 19 November 1985, when 54-2809 returned to Davis-Monthan once again for storage and ultimate disposal, as the Air Force completed its phase-out of the type.

Although the thirteen-month restoration culminated in a beautiful example of the restorer's art, the owners chose to have the aircraft completed in an anonymous, more generic USAF scheme, rather than any of its previous units' markings. This was to show the C-131 as representative of the entire Air Force fleet, and their varying roles through their almost-forty-year continuous service, rather than identifying the aircraft with any one particular unit.

Once the airframe work had been completed, attention was turned to the interior, which was stripped bare in preparation for a complete refurbishment. Barry wanted his C-131 to show the many different roles performed by the Convair during its long and varied USAF career, complete with installation of original fittings from Air Force C-131s and T-29s. The forward section of the passenger cabin was furnished with VIP seating, representing the role of this particular aircraft and the many other similarly appointed staff transport C-131Ds. In the rear cabin examples of other roles undertaken by the type in military service are represented. In the rear cabin two patient-stretchers and accompanying equipment represent the emergency air-evacuation role, and the centre section the bombardier/navigator training role carried out by the Air Force's Convair T-29s. The navigator stations were acquired from a T-29 on display in a museum in Calhoun, Georgia, and are seen here during fitting in October 1997. One of the stretchers was taken from a derelict C-131 in Western's yard, whilst the second was sourced from a local Army-surplus store.

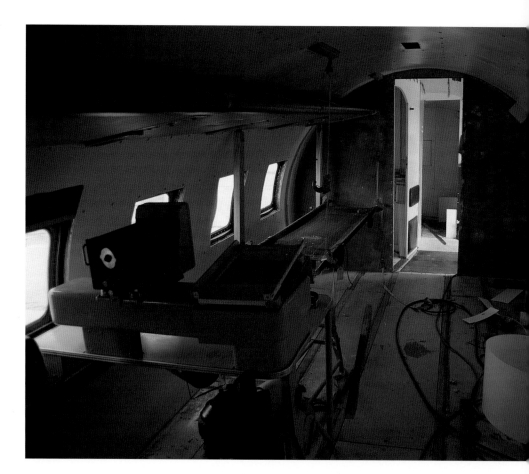

A total of 515 military Convairs were produced for the US Air Force and Navy, of which 390 were based on the Model 240 airframe, covering four different T-29 variants and the original transport version, the C-131A. The larger and much improved Model 340 was the platform for all subsequent deliveries, C-131B/C/D/E models for the Air Force and the R4Y-1 and -2 for the Navy, later redesignated C-131F. The USAF C-131D was based wholly upon the commercial Model 340 and delivered with a standard 44-seat passenger interior. In reality, the deliveries were made up of both 340 and 440 airframes, as a number of the original batch were diverted to commercial customers.

The forward cabin of 54-2809 is restored to how it would have been when delivered from Convair's San Diego factory, back in 1954, and includes a fully furnished and operative galley station between the passenger cabin and flight deck. This view, looking forward, shows the quality of refurbishment undertaken by Western International in returning the C-131 to its original condition.

Convair had been the main rival to the Glenn L. Martin Company throughout the 1950s. The Model 240 had been in competition with the troublesome Martin 2-0-2 though, being unpressurised, it was soon overtaken by the more advanced Martin 4-0-4. This lead was soon arrested, when Convair introduced its larger and much improved 340/440 series, which did much to stifle the Martin 4-0-4. With a very similar layout and identical powerplants, the Convair and Martin products were pitted square against one another for

business in the lucrative domestic US market, as many major carriers looked to upgrade from older, war-surplus equipment. Although on paper the Convair was not able to outperform its rival from Baltimore, it won hands down on passenger comfort, boasting a more spacious interior than the Martin equivalent.

With the introduction into service in the United States of the Vickers Viscount, airline passengers were becoming aware of the smoother and quieter ride afforded by

turbine power. In a bid to improve its passenger appeal, Convair initiated a number of modifications to the Model 340. These included considerable effort to reduce cabin noise and vibration, especially in the forward cabin. The only external changes involved closer-fitting engine cowls and replacing the twin engine exhaust stacks with a new, rectangular exhaust outlet. These modifications were incorporated into all USAF airframes during production, as illustrated in this view.

Classic Wings' C-131D restoration has broken new ground, both in the American warbird movement and amongst owners and operators of classic post-war commercial aircraft, and may bring about the adoption of other, more unusual, restoration projects in the future. At this time, at least two other organisations in the United States are planning restorations on Convair 240 and turbine 580 airframes. In Australia, the world-acclaimed Historical Aircraft Restoration Society (HARS) is planning a full restoration of an ex-USAF C-131D, to represent a Convair 340 operated by an Australian domestic airline.

Here, as pilot Chuck Clapper breaks the Convair away from the T-6 photo plane at the end of the air-to-air sortie exclusively arranged for this book, the simple and clean lines of the Convair are well illustrated. In early 2002 Classic Wings sold its immaculate Convair to the Southern California Wing of the CAF, where it joined C-46 *China Doll* at its Camarillo base.

BEST OF BRITISH

British innovation and technology have always been in the forefront of aviation and, more often than not, accompanied by style and beauty.

The distinctive and romantic view that could only come from a de Havilland. Sir Geoffrey de Havilland was responsible for many of the UK's most advanced and successful aircraft designs, from the simple appeal of the family of Moth biplanes to the world-beating Comet jet airliner. His innovation was accompanied by a realisation that aircraft need not be solely functional, they could also be endowed with style and beauty. The tapered biplane wings, struts and bracing wires define the beauty that is the DH-89 Dragon Rapide.

Hugely popular in its day, the Rapide was developed from the DH-86 Dragon, a four-engined model of slightly larger dimensions, and became the last wooden biplane produced by de Havilland. The prototype first flew in April 1934 and over the next ten years 730 examples were built, many of which were put into service with Commonwealth countries at the outbreak of World War Two.

The Rapide remained in production for ten years, becoming one of the most widely used transport types in the world at the time. Powered by two de Havilland Gipsy Queen six-cylinder inverted inline engines, the Rapide was capable of a top speed of 157 mph and a ceiling of 19,000 ft. Later variants were fitted with trailing-edge flaps on the lower wing to improve performance.

For wartime use a number of examples were converted for combat operations, with a Vickers machine-gun fitted in the starboard nose and a small bomb bay for two 100 lb and four 20 lb bombs. The type's military career, however, mainly involved liaison and transport duties or navigation training, in the case of the de Havilland Dominie. The last Royal Air Force

Dominies were declared redundant in 1955, though one or two remained on charge until early 1961. This beautifully restored example is owned and operated by William Gray of Auckland, New Zealand in a latter-day RAF scheme. (*Gordon Bain*)

The Rapide's narrow cabin was able to carry a full load of up to ten passengers, though most operated with a maximum of eight seats for passenger comfort. The single-seat flight deck was visible to the front-seat passengers, affording them views forward over the pilot's shoulder. The Dragon Rapide is one of the best-loved pre-war aircraft and, in its heyday, was loved by the rich and famous including Edward VIII, then Prince of Wales, who kept one at his disposal. Today its style makes it one of the most graceful vintage aircraft still flying.

The genteel flying characteristics of the Rapide are still available to the public, with a number of operators offering pleasure flights in their beautifully restored aircraft. One such company is Classic Wings, whose Duxford-based operation has two wonderfully restored examples that fly regularly throughout summer weekends.

Classic Wings' Rapides have been meticulously restored to comply with modern regulations with seating for eight passengers in a style few air travellers can remember. G-AIYR *Classic Lady* began operating in late 1990 and, in its stylish period green-and-cream livery, can regularly be seen operating from Duxford's flight line throughout the summer.

Probably one of the most unique and unusual British classics still airworthy is the wonderful Short Sandringham flying-boat owned by Kermit Weeks. Based at Weeks's unique Fantasy of Flight aviation theme park in Florida, the Sandringham is the only airworthy example of its kind and represents the last word in luxury, pre-war air travel. The Short Sandringham was a post-war civil conversion of the wartime Sunderland patrol bomber. The conversion involved removal of front and rear turrets and replacing them with streamlined fairings, whilst the interior was refurbished to hold up to thirty passengers in luxury

that was reminiscent of an ocean-going liner, including two passenger decks, a promenade deck, cocktail bar and restaurant. Twenty-six examples were converted, with the first civilian conversion flying in 1946.

Weeks's unique flying-boat was last flown commercially by Antilles Air Boats in the Virgin Islands as VP-LVF. Purchased by Edward Hulton in May 1979 and registered N158J, it set off from St Croix in November 1980 for the epic Atlantic crossing which, after seven months, was completed when it arrived at its new home in Marseilles on 24 May 1981. Re-registered G-BJHS, the

Sandringham did little flying in Europe, later spending some time at Calshot in the UK where, after much uncertainty over its future, it underwent extensive renovation following its sale to Kermit Weeks. Following a number of test flights, the Sandringham finally left UK waters on 20 July 1993, bound for the USA. With *en route* stops in Ireland, Reykjavik and Goose Bay, Labrador, it finally splashed down at Lake Winnebago, at the EAA Convention in Oshkosh, eight days later. From there, the aircraft was ferried to its permanent home in Florida, where it is seen at rest on the water at Polk City.

The Avro Anson, named after the eighteenth-century Royal Navy Admiral, George Anson, was originally designed as a light, four-passenger civil transport and the first three were built for Imperial Airways in 1935. However, the British Air Ministry soon recognised the potential of the simple twin-engined design to fulfil a number of military roles, principally as a coastal patrol and reconnaissance aircraft. The first examples entered service with the RAF and RAAF in 1936, becoming the first operational aircraft with retractable landing gear. However, even with an enclosed gun turret, two internally carried 100 lb bombs, and external racks that could carry eight 20 lb bombs, flares or smoke generators, the type was soon found to be severely under-armed for this role, and was eventually replaced by the Lockheed Hudson. With an active service life that extended from 1936 to 1952, more than 11,000 Ansons were built and one was still flying for the RAF in 1968.

Today, there are but three examples still

airworthy, one operated in Canada by Canadian Warplane Heritage and two in the UK. Famed air transport operator Air Atlantique is the owner of the beautifully restored WD413, which was returned to flight in February 1998, and is seen here during an early post-restoration flight from its Coventry base.

Anson WD413 was one of 252 Mk 21s built, from a total UK production run of over 8,000 between 1936 and 1952; a further 2,882 were produced in Canada. This aircraft was manufactured at A. V. Roe's Yeadon plant in 1950 as a T. Mk 21 and first served with the Air Navigation School at RAF Hullavington in January 1951, following a short period of storage at Silloth with 22 Maintenance Unit (MU). Returned to Silloth in June 1953, thence to Avro for conversion to C. Mk 21, WD413

was returned to service with the RAF Bomber Command Communications Flight at Booker in March 1955. Further transfers, between April 1958 and July 1963 saw WD413 operating with the Communications Flights of Fighter Command and later Transport Command in July 1963, before finally being retired to 23 MU at Aldergrove in 1965. Given the maintenance serial 7881M, the Anson was then employed as a maintenance training aid.

In December 1977 it was registered to

Mr G. M. K. Fraser as G-BFIR and returned to flying status soon afterwards. The Anson was flown to its new base at East Midlands Airport, where it is seen on a damp June morning in 1978, still wearing its latter-day RAF colours with high-visibility dayglo fuselage and tail markings, which were typical of many RAF training aircraft in the late 1960s. (*Keith Gaskell*)

During the following years the Anson was repainted in slightly updated RAF markings and appeared at numerous airshows throughout the UK, operating from its new base at White Waltham. However, during an air display at Andrewsfield in summer 1981 it suffered slight damage, when a brake-cylinder failure caused it to ground-loop on landing. A protracted period of repairs then ensued, which saw the aircraft moved between East Midlands, Hurn, RAF Turnhouse and, finally, Strathallan in 1987. During 1993 the Anson was moved yet again, first to Teesside, then Enstone before eventually arriving at Lee-on-Solent to be restored to airworthiness once again. The Aircraft Restoration Company at Duxford took on the final stages of WD413's restoration in July 1996, including a full repaint and acquiring the necessary permit to fly from the CAA.

Tuesday 17 February 1998 saw a very proud Captain Mike Collett, chairman of the Air Atlantique Group, pilot the Anson from Duxford to its new home at Coventry, where soon afterwards the appropriate marks G-VROE were allocated. The aircraft now takes pride of place amongst the Group's varied fleet of former RAF types.

The Anson was of very conventional design and construction, the wing was made of spruce and Bakelite-bonded plywood and its fuselage of steel tube with fabric and plywood covering. Powered by two 310 hp Armstrong Siddeley Cheetah air-cooled radial engines, the Anson was rather pedestrian in performance, capable of only 190 mph at maximum power, with a maximum range of only 790 miles. Initially intended to be the standard twin-engined pilot trainer for the British Commonwealth Air Training Plan (BCATP), the Anson was also used for training radio operators, navigators, and bombardiers. After the war many former military examples were converted for civilian use, though production for commercial customers resumed with the Anson Mk X. This variant was completed with a strengthened cabin floor for freight and passenger use, whilst later models had enlarged passenger cabins, through a raised cabin roof, for passenger comfort, and all-metal wings. A civilian variety of the Anson, the Avro 19, was produced using a Mk XI airframe and manufactured in limited quantities for British internal routes. The Anson was eventually replaced in airline service during the post-war years by larger, more capable aircraft, though the type remained popular with many second-level operators.

One airline, whose humble beginnings were built around a small fleet of Avro Ansons, chose to celebrate its 50th anniversary in style by commemorating the founding of the airline in appropriate fashion. Today, Gulf Air is a major international carrier, with a varied fleet of modern wide-body airliners, though, as Gulf Aviation the company was registered in London in 1950 to operate an air service, based in Bahrain, in support of oil exploration work in the Middle East. Equipped with two Austers and a single Anson, Gulf Aviation began operations in March of that year. Expansion quickly followed, as three further examples were put into service, alongside a number of de Havilland DH-86Bs before more-modern types began to take over, with the introduction of the de Havilland Dove into the fleet in 1951.

Air Atlantique's beautiful Anson, G-VROE, was painted to represent the airline's first aircraft, G-AIWX, as part of Gulf Air's anniversary celebrations. The Anson, accompanied by a suitably repainted Dove, also from Air Atlantique,

flew from Coventry airport through Europe and the Middle East, to Bahrain, where they became the centre-piece of the airline's celebrations. The five-week journey began on 10 March 2000, with *en route* stops at Nevers in France; Genoa and Naples in Italy. At the next stop, Corfu, a minor hydraulic snag delayed the flight by three days but the aircraft continued through Santorini and Heraklion to Alexandria, in Egypt, where engine problems again held things up slightly. Finally, on 23 March, following further stops in Luxor, Jedda and Riyadh, both aircraft made a nostalgic flypast at Bahrain and landed to an ecstatic crowd.

Another uniquely British design which, despite its outstanding performance, never enjoyed a hugely successful commercial career, is the Scottish Aviation Twin Pioneer. The twin-engined development of Scottish Aviation Limited's original Pioneer design inherited all of the unique STOL (Short Take-off and Landing) performance of its predecessor, coupled with an increased payload and range. First flown in June 1955, the type showed immense potential for both commercial and military operators. However, the second prototype was destroyed in a fatal crash, caused by catastrophic wing failure, which did much to dampen the enthusiasm for the type. The accident further compounded the misfortunes of the Twin Pioneer, as SAL's Managing Director David McIntyre, who was a major driving force in the company's business, and in aviation in general at the time, was killed in the crash. The company did eventually go on to produce eighty-nine 'Twin Pins', favoured by airlines and air forces whose operations were conducted in the more rugged regions of the world.

The last airworthy example in the UK is owned and operated by Air Atlantique, from its Coventry airport base. G-APRS was originally operated by the manufacturer as a demonstrator before being sold to the UK's Empire Test Pilots' School (ETPS) in 1965, gaining the military serial XT610. Retired from service life in February 1975, it was re-registered G-BCWF and enjoyed a short career with an aerial survey company before coming to Air Atlantique in 1992. After a thorough overhaul it first appeared in the airline's green livery, restored to its original identity, before being repainted in the markings seen here, which are based upon the current ETPS scheme, though not as worn by the aircraft when operated by the unit.

As well as operating varied fleets of commercial freight and passenger aircraft, Air Atlantique excels in the restoration and operation of a rich fleet of classic British aircraft. Founder and company chairman Mike Collett is deservedly proud of the company's unique fleet, which is housed at Atlantique's Coventry headquarters. Included in this valuable collection is this beautifully restored de Havilland Dove, appropriately registered G-DHDV, seen here in period Gulf Air livery after taking part in the airline's 50th anniversary celebrations in 2000. Strictly speaking, this is a Devon C. Mk 1, the military variant of de Havilland's popular post-war commuter airliner. Delivered to the Air Force in January 1949 as VP981, it operated variously with the Station Flight at RAF Hendon and as personal mount of the British Air Attaché in Paris. It was also flown on behalf of the Commander of the Allied Air Forces of Central Europe as well as operating with Nos 21 and 207 Squadrons RAF. Latterly, the Devon was

flown as support aircraft for the RAF's Battle of Britain Memorial Flight before being acquired by Air Atlantique.

In today's harsh business climate, operating a fully functional flying museum

alongside numerous commercial air transport companies is a very bold venture. Long may Air Atlantique's pioneering efforts in vintage aircraft restoration and operation continue.

Another of de Havilland's distinctive transports, the DH-114 Heron, is slightly less well represented amongst the numbers of restored classics currently flying, with only a handful still airworthy. The Dove had been conceived as a natural successor to the Dragon Rapide; similarly, the Heron was intended to replace the four-engined DH-86 feederliner. Although the Heron was conceived soon after the end of World War Two, de Havilland postponed its development for a few years, allowing the market to develop sufficiently before proceeding with the design. Essentially a scaled-up Dove, with four 250-hp Gipsy Queen engines, the type was envisaged for short-field operations and use in underdeveloped countries. First flown in May 1950, with fixed undercarriage, the improved Mk 2 was later introduced with fully retractable gear and improved, supercharged engines giving the Heron a respectable cruise speed of 190 mph over a range of 915 miles. Production totalled 148 airframes, though the type did enjoy an extended career through numerous re-engining programmes as well as being the basis of the radically modified Saunders ST-27 conversion, with twin turbine engines.

This beautifully restored example is flown from its base at Jersey in the Channel Islands by Duchess of Brittany (Jersey) Ltd, in the colours of Jersey Airlines, which operated seven examples from 1955 until the airline merged with British United Airways in 1962. This example was originally built for British European Airways in May 1956, at the time Jersey Airlines reached an agreement with BEA to consolidate its Channel Island services and acquired two of BEA's Herons. Flown as *Duchess of Brittany*, G-AORG operated on a

busy route network radiating from Guernsey to Alderney, Southampton and Dinard, as well as other destinations in northern France and the UK. Sold in March 1961 to the Ministry of Defence, it was allocated the serial XR441 and flown by the Fleet Air Arm, ending its service days with RNAS Yeovilton Station Flight. Finally retired in December 1989, it was placed in temporary storage at RAF Shawbury until acquired by its present owners in May the following year and restored to its former glory. (*Martin E. Siegrist*)

The de Havilland Aircraft Company Ltd spawned a number of foreign subsidiary companies which, over the years, designed and developed many aircraft specific to their own markets. The de Havilland DHA-3 Drover is one such design, a product of de Havilland Aircraft Pty. Ltd, Australia and intended as a replacement for the ageing DH-84 Dragon. Conceived in 1946, the type's unusual design is of similar dimensions to the DH-104 Dove and came about after consideration that the twin-engined Dove was seen as not rugged enough for the challenging conditions of Australia's outback.

De Havilland Australia, instead, opted for a three-engine layout with a fixed tail-wheel undercarriage. Powered by three 145-hp Gipsy Major engines, considerably lighter than the Dove's twin 330-hp layout, the prototype Drover, VH-DHA, first took flight on 23 January 1948. Intended for commercial operation by Qantas, the type's early engine problems caused a series of bad accidents, which quickly tarnished its image with the airline, and its examples were soon disposed of.

In seven years of production only twenty examples were built, and all but one aircraft were sold to the airlines, the Department of Civil Aviation or the Royal Flying Doctor Service. Nowadays, there are only two airworthy examples in Australia, with a number of survivors displayed in various museums throughout the country, as well as one in a British museum. This unique formation, specially arranged for inclusion in this book features VH-DHM, one of the last of the type to be built, now owned by Hawker de Havilland in Sydney and operated on the company's behalf by the Historic Aircraft Restoration Society, together with the privately owned VH-ADN.

The beautifully restored VH-ADN is owned and operated by Peter Hanneman and Charlie Camilleri from Bathurst airport in New South Wales, Australia. It first flew on 31 October 1951 as VH-EBT, built for Qantas for use in Papua New Guinea. It was later sold to Fiji Airlines as VQ-FAP and eventually returned to Australia in 1961, where it took up the marks VH-ADN and was operated by Lindeman Island Airways until 1969. Subsequent owners of this Drover were Jim Hazleton, Southern Cross Parachutes and later John and Helen Brown in Morwell, Victoria, until sale to its present owners in 1999. The Drover, which exemplifies Australia's indigenous post-war aircraft industry, is flown regularly and presently has little over 12,220 hours on the clock.

HEAVY METAL

Against all odds, the numbers of airworthy large piston-powered types continue to grow. Some of these superb restorations are featured on the following pages, together with a selection of others that may be restored in the future.

A sight so familiar to airline passengers a generation ago: the popular saying of the time 'Trust in God and Pratt & Whitney' comes to mind in this glorious view of a pair of R-2800 radials seen from the cabin window of a Douglas DC-6. Ousted from commercial service by the introduction of jet airliners in the late 1950s, the DC-6 was the backbone of many major operators' long-haul fleets for more than a decade. Many second-tier carriers and charter airlines still enjoyed the pleasures of the DC-6 well into the early 1970s and, even today, the type remains in service on cargo operations throughout the world.

Even though much more successful than the Lockheed Constellation, the Douglas DC-6 was always relegated into second place where looks and charisma were concerned. Perhaps this could explain the reason that the Connie has prevailed with a future after commercial operation, with the handful of examples restored to full airworthiness and operated under private ownership. In Tucson, Arizona, during the late 1980s, however, one big Douglas did enjoy a short life in the limelight in private ownership. The aircraft, one of the oldest and last US military examples operated, had enjoyed a celebrated career, ending its service life as a VIP transport operated by the Headquarters of the United States Marine Corps. Tucson resident Tony De Alissandri's Lan-Dale Corporation acquired VC-118B Bu. No. 128427 from desert storage at Davis-Monthan AFB on 1 August 1986, the aircraft having spent only four years in store. Finished in the Corps' red and gold trim, this particular C-118 was probably one of the most luxurious examples operated by the US military. Fully restored to its original condition and appropriately registered N427D, its new owners took great pride in its operation though the aircraft was seldom flown, not least due to the immense running costs in sustaining four thirsty 18-cylinder radial engines. The aircraft was eventually donated to the USMC for display at its last operational base, MCAS Cherry Point, North Carolina.

The UK presently has the only commercially operated DC-6s in Europe, with two examples flown by Atlantic Airlines on *ad hoc* freight work. Now, however, some twenty years since the last passenger-configured DC-6 operated in Europe, an example has recently been acquired by an Austrian organisation with the sole intention of carrying out passenger pleasure-flying, allowing many the joyous experience of air travel in an ageing, charismatic propliner. Operated by 'The Flying Bulls', the flight division of the manufacturer of the famous energy drink Red Bull, the aircraft is the former Namibian Commercial Aviation DC-6B, V5-NCF, which was acquired in May 2000 after a long search by the organisation for a suitable aircraft. The second-to-last DC-6 to be built, this aircraft was originally delivered to the Yugoslavian state carrier Jugoslovenski Aerotransport in October 1958 and was later one of two operated by the Yugoslav Air Force as Government VIP transports.

Ferried from its last home at Windhoek in Namibia, where it flew tourist passenger charters until its surprise retirement in early 2000, the aircraft arrived at Salzburg on 10 July 2000 at the end of its three-day delivery flight, which was completed without any problem. The DC-6B routed via Victoria Falls; Entebbe, Uganda and Luxor, Egypt before leaving Africa for the last time to cruise over the Greek Islands and, after transiting Italian airspace, it arrived in Austria on a midsummer's afternoon to a jubilant welcome from a huge crowd of well-wishers. A full refurbishment of the airframe, engines and interior will be undertaken before the aircraft takes flight again, expected to be during 2003. (*Michael Prophet*)

In Oakland, California another former military DC-6 is the subject of a lengthy and ambitious restoration programme which will, hopefully, see this old-timer restored to a representative example of those flown by United Airlines on its world-wide route network. This particular aircraft was rolled out of Douglas's Long Beach plant in August 1955 and delivered to the USAF as C-118A, 53-3279, where it operated as part of the combined Military Air Transport Service. In 1966 it received a posting to Europe, joining the ranks of the 439

Military Airlift Group at Frankfurt-Main air base in Germany, where it remained based until June 1972, when it was transferred to the 1701 Air Base Wing at Wiesbaden to see out its Air Force days. Retired to desert storage in 1975, it was resurrected the following year when reassigned to the US Navy for operation with Navy Logistic Support Squadron VR-52 at Willow Grove Naval Air Station in Pennsylvania. Here it served its final days until retirement in February 1985.

Sold at public auction three years later,

the Douglas acquired the civilian registration N578AS and was soon caught up in a rather unsavoury chapter, following its entry into civilian life. At least one less-than-legal cargo operation resulted in the C-118 being seized by the US Drug Enforcement Agency and impounded at Fort Lauderdale International airport, Florida. At this time another former US Navy C-118 was also present on the airport and it appeared that the identities of both aircraft may have been transposed, adding further confusion to the situation.

By the late 1990s the C-118 had been acquired by Miami-based Nighthawk Air Services and moved to another part of the airport, where restoration to full airworthiness by the group Radial Reminiscence was planned. This group began restoring the C-118 for a flight to Oakland, California, where a full restoration was planned, to represent one of United Airlines' 'Mainliner' DC-6A fleet of the 1950s. United Airlines received its first DC-6, along with American Airlines, in a combined ceremony on 24 November 1946. However, as the type was still awaiting its FAA certificate of airworthiness, commercial passenger operations were delayed for five more months, allowing the airlines to complete crew training and route proving flights prior to their introduction into service. Once the formalities were concluded United's DC-6s were soon in direct competition with TWA's Constellations on the major US transcontinental routes.

Once at Oakland, N578AS was stripped of all its original paint and preparations were made for the application of period United Airlines markings. Thus far,

however, only the port side has been finished, and restoration work has slowed down considerably, as this October 1999 view shows.

The markings of the other original customer of the type, American Airlines, can still be seen on an airworthy DC-6 in the United States, though in a very different role from that originally intended. Aerial fire-fighting specialist TBM operates this immaculately turned-out example, the only one of its type now operating in this role in the US. The aircraft, N90739, is an original, short-fuselage American Airlines DC-6 and was delivered to the airline in October 1947 as *Flagship Georgia*. After almost twenty years of sterling service the aircraft was sold in November 1966 to aircraft broker F. B. Ayer & Associates for conversion to DC-6F freighter. Acquired the following year by Miami Aviation Corporation, the aircraft was later leased by The Monkees pop group in the late 1960s to support one of their concert tours. Later sold to Dallas Aero Services, the DC-6 was eventually flown to Greater Southwest airport, Fort Worth, Texas, during 1970 for storage, and put up for sale. In 1973 TBM purchased the freighter and began its conversion to air-tanker. The aircraft was allocated the identity 'Tanker 97' by the United States Forestry Service.

To the casual observer, the DC-6 was outwardly similar to its predecessor the DC-4; however, the type was very different in many aspects. Conscious of wartime restrictions, Douglas was keen to press ahead with an improved version of the C-54/DC-4 and succeeded in securing the military's interest and funding for the project with the Skymaster Improvement Programme, which allowed the production of three prototypes of this new aircraft. Based upon the C-54E variant, the successful type was designated XC-112A. Although retaining the same wing design as the DC-4, the new type featured a lengthened and fully pressurised fuselage with square passenger-cabin windows, whilst longer engine nacelles housed more-powerful Pratt & Whitney R-2800 Twin Wasp engines.

Although too late for any military career, the XC-112 paved the way for Douglas's return to commercial business and quickly gained acceptance with the airlines. As joint launch customer, American Airlines introduced DC-6s wearing the carrier's

distinctive 'lightning bolt' logo on the New York to Chicago route in April 1947. Now, more than fifty years later, it is amazing to see an American Airlines 'original' still sporting its original livery, although operating in a completely different environment. Nowadays, *Flagship Georgia* can be seen working the fire-lines in the Pacific Northwest of the USA, on contract to the USFS as 'Tanker 68'.

The famous American Airlines livery can also be seen adorning yet another 'unique' big Douglas in the United States: once again, an original American Airlines aircraft restored to its former markings, as worn when it was delivered to the airline in March 1956. Turks Air's DC-7BF, N381AA is the only one of its kind flown commercially anywhere in the world on cargo work. Sadly, like many of its contemporaries, the DC-7 enjoyed an all too brief time in the limelight as one of the last examples of its breed, soon to be superseded by the introduction of jets.

This DC-7 had languished at Opa Locka airport, in southern Florida for a number of years, the property of Alaskan freight company Brooks Fuel. Following negotiations between Brooks and Carlos Gomez, owner of Turks Air, a deal was concluded for the DC-7 in late 1998 and work began on its restoration to flying status which, by the end of September the following year, was close to complete. The DC-7, like the Lockheed Constellation, acquired a reputation for troublesome engines and, true to form, Carlos's DC-7 was no different. Even after having all four

Wright R-3350s overhauled, an engine failed during routine engine runs, necessitating an expensive zero-time replacement. Problems persisted which required further cylinder changes before all was well enough to perform its first flight in many years. Thankfully, Turks Air's DC-7 has since gained a reputation for reliability and versatility which can rival any of the jet cargo operators in the region, and is now gainfully employed on regular freight work from southern Florida to various destinations in the Caribbean. (*Michael Prophet*)

The fondness of returning classic types to their original period liveries has also been embraced by Chandler, Arizona-based International Air Response, whose immaculate DC-7B has recently undergone a transformation back to its original Delta Air Lines scheme. Owner Woody Grantham has long been associated with the DC-7 and his last operational example, N4887C, has flown on contract to the State of Alaska as 'Tanker 33' for the past few years. At the end of the 1999 season, the aircraft was stripped of its previous red and black livery during winter maintenance in preparation for its return to glory, as seen here.

The aircraft was one of ten originally delivered to Delta, being handed over in November 1957. The DC-7 spent a little over ten years with the airline, operating on its 'Royal' services, as the various flights were named, including the 'Royal Caribe' service to San Juan, Puerto Rico and Caracas, Venezuela, the first intercontinental service by the type. Eventually sold to broker BMR Aviation in March 1968, it was quickly sold on to the Washington D.C.-based Emerald Shillelagh Air Travel Club which operated it for the next five years. Finally, after another brief period with another travel club, its present owner, then known as T & G Aviation, acquired it in mid-1980.

Coincidentally, a second ex-Delta Air Lines DC-7B also resides at Chandler and, although in a poor condition now, it is hoped that one day it too can shine like its former fleet-mate. This example, N4889C, was formerly fleet number '719' with Delta, delivered from Long Beach in late December 1957. Delta's DC-7s were operated variously in 69-seat first-class configuration to 90-seat coach-class seating layout towards the end of their career and were the final piston-engined types ordered by the airline.

Like its fleet-mates, '719' served for only a short time with Delta, being sold to the Atlanta Skylarks Travel Club in 1966, which flew the aircraft until 1973. Following a brief tenure with another organisation, Aerial Applicators Inc. eventually acquired the DC-7 in 1975, a move which secured its future, saving it from the sad demise faced by so many of its contemporaries, which were rendered redundant by the introduction of jets to the world's airline fleets. The aircraft was never actually converted to aerial applicator or air-tanker configuration, instead it remained grounded at Chandler, donating engines and airframe parts to

other, more fortunate examples. The aircraft's fortunes may yet take a turn for the better, however, as in recent years two different organisations with intentions of restoration have expressed an interest in the airframe.

Complex engines and airframes of ageing piston-powered transports seem to present no problem for certain specialist operators, such as Hawkins & Powers, Aviation Inc. The Wyoming-based air-tanker operator has long been associated with a sizeable fleet of large and exotic types containing the last remaining examples of a number of World War Two bombers and transport aircraft. As well as the last flying examples of the wartime PB4Y Privateer Navy Patrol Bomber, the company also owns the world's sole airworthy Fairchild C-82 Packet, which it recently restored. The C-119 Flying Boxcar, developed from the Packet, is a type which became synonymous with H & P during the 1970s, as the company began to expand its fire-fighting capacity, owning more than a dozen airframes at one time. The final examples were retired from operation in the early 1980s and many were donated to aviation museums across the United States.

The company maintains a healthy interest in the restoration and preservation of classic aircraft and one C-119 was eventually resurrected to flying status and displayed by the company at the EAA Airventure at Oshkosh. The aircraft concerned, N8093, a former RCAF C-119G, had last flown in the production of the movie *Always* and its return to flight status was completed in late 1997. It is seen at its Greybull, Wyoming base in October of that year, towards the end of its restoration.

Opposite: Even though they represented the pinnacle of propeller-engined airliner technology, the Douglas DC-7 and Lockheed Constellation were never given the opportunity to shine and realise their immense potential. Engine and airframe developments on both designs succeeded in increasing performance well beyond that originally anticipated when the first examples entered service. Such performance, however, was not achieved without problems and on numerous occasions both types were referred to as the best three-engined airliners ever to fly, given that both the DC-7 and Constellation used the powerful, but troublesome, Wright R-3350 engine. Nowadays, the airworthy Constellation fleet is made up entirely of privately owned and operated examples, its commercial days now over. The DC-7, by comparison, continues to serve, albeit in small numbers, in both the freight and air-tanker roles in the United States.

The glorious sight and sound of four mighty Wright radials at maximum power is a very evocative experience, as demonstrated here by TBM's DC-7B, N838D, as it roars off the William J. Fox Field's runway in October 1999. Built for Eastern Airlines in 1958, the aircraft enjoyed a short career with the airline, being sold some eight years later, another victim of the jet age.

Whilst not the easiest aircraft to maintain, and certainly one of the more expensive to operate, the C-119 has, nevertheless, proved attractive to a number of private organisations over the years. One former USAF example was privately operated for a while in the early 1980s, whilst the Mid Atlantic Air Museum, famous for its first-class restorations of two ex-US Navy P-2 Neptunes and a Martin 4-0-4 airliner, acquired C-119F N175ML in 1995. The aircraft was flown to the museum's Reading, Pennsylvania site in December of that year, following a lengthy restoration in Arizona, where the aircraft had been parked up for a number of years. The aircraft, formerly US Marines Bu. No. 131677, had been the last of its type operated by the Marines when, in July 1975, it was retired and flown to Davis-Monthan AFB for storage and eventual disposal. Sold in June 1980 to DMI, a salvage and reclamation company, the aircraft remained in storage with DMI until acquired by the Marine Lumber Company of Nantucket. Stripped of its military markings, the aircraft saw little, if any, service before being flown to Avra Valley airport in Arizona, parked up and once again offered for sale. The Mid Atlantic Air Museum finally concluded a deal to acquire the C-119 in 1995, and has long-term plans to restore it to original USMC markings and operate the aircraft as part of the museum's active fleet.

The Mid Atlantic Air Museum is also responsible for an ambitious and long-term restoration project, intended to recognise and celebrate one type which, in its day, represented the cutting edge of commercial air travel. The Vickers Viscount is poorly represented in aviation museums throughout the world, given that it was the very first, commercial turbine-engined airliner to enter regular airline service, paving the way for countless subsequent designs. MAAM acquired Vickers V.798D Viscount, N555SL, in 1992 when it was donated by Tony Abad, who had purchased it from Monarch Airlines of Chino, California. The Viscount had been dormant at Chino after retirement by Monarch, which had operated it as a freighter to distribute the *Wall Street Journal* throughout the US west-coast region. Flown from Chino in August 1992 to Clarksburg, West

Virginia, the Viscount was restored and repainted in its original Capital Airlines scheme and took up its first assigned marks of N7471, one of the last batch of ten series 745D airframes built for the airline in the late 1950s. At that time, Capital was in financial difficulties and Vickers chose to retain these aircraft until another buyer could be found. This was an unfortunate situation as Capital, the first airline to recognise the quality and performance of the type, had championed the Viscount's cause in the United States, as a result of which many other operators soon followed. After a year in storage the aircraft, now modified to a series 798D, was delivered to Northeast Airlines as N6591C in August 1958. Sold in 1964, the Viscount was converted to VIP configuration and entered a new career as a corporate transport, originally as N820BK with Blaw-Knox

Corporation and later with Kearney & Trecker who re-registered it N1898T. Eventually purchased by Monarch, the Viscount was stripped of its interior fittings and operated in freight configuration.

Shortly after the museum received the Viscount, contamination of the fuel system was discovered, following a number of engine problems whilst returning from an airlines convention and Capital Airlines Association reunion in Washington D.C. This situation led to the decision to fully overhaul the airframe, including the fuel system, and restore it to full airworthy, passenger configuration. This has now been under way since the mid-1990s, the long and expensive process presently being delayed by the need to acquire a replacement number-one engine, which 'self-destructed' whilst engine-running in 1998. (*John Proctor*)

Probably one of the most ambitious restoration projects currently under way is the Berlin Airlift Historic Foundation's mammoth task of restoring and operating a mighty Boeing C-97 Stratofreighter. This 'beast' amongst propliners, one of the most powerful propeller-driven transports to enter service, was also one of the most complex and costly to maintain, thanks due in no small part to the four massive Pratt & Whitney R-4360 engines. The 'Strat' has a look all its own, thanks to the distinctive 'double-bubble' fuselage design, favoured by Boeing as giving greater strength against pressurisation over the more conventional single-lobe fuselage designs of other manufacturers. This feature would become common on Boeing's subsequent jet designs, the distinctive join of the upper and lower lobes being masked by the outer skin. The C-97, or Boeing Model 367, to use the manufacturer's designation, was a cargo/transport development of the B-29 Superfortress, retaining the bomber's wings, tail, undercarriage and, on early models, its engines. To the original B-29 fuselage was added a second, upper fuselage lobe to give the required cargo capacity, thus producing the type's distinctive look.

BAHF's Strat was built for the USAF as a KC-97G, 52-2718, part of the second contract placed with Boeing in fiscal year 1952 for this variant, the most numerous of the six different models produced, accounting for 592 of the 888 C-97s built. The KC-97G was the air-refuelling tanker version of the Strat, dispensing fuel through Boeing's unique 'flying boom' apparatus under the lower rear fuselage. In its heyday, Strategic Air Command operated ten fully equipped strategic bomber wings, with a complement of up to twenty KC-97s assigned to each unit. A number of these aircraft were later modified to KC-97L configuration, by the Hayes International Corporation, which included the fitting of two under-wing General Electric J-47 jets, to augment their performance in the tanking role. In its transport role, the C-97 utilised twin clam-shell loading doors under the rear fuselage and an upward-opening forward side-cargo door opening into the cavernous hold.

The aircraft ended its Air Force service with the Utah Air National Guard (ANG) at Salt Lake City airport and was retired in September 1976. Sold in July 1981 from Davis-Monthan AFB, one of thirteen KC-97Ls acquired by Kolar Inc., it was registered N117GA and flown to nearby Tucson airport where it remained, inactive, for the next few years. It finally left Tucson in October 1989 upon sale to the Grace Aire Foundation Inc., a charitable trust registered in Corpus Christi, Texas, which used the aircraft on airborne relief and aid work, which involved visits to Central and South America and the Caribbean. This work was interspersed with occasional lucrative freight charter work in Alaska until 1995, when the Strat was ferried to Moses Lake, Washington awaiting further work or a possible new owner.

In civil guise, the Boeing B-377 Stratocruiser was not the most successful of airliners, with only six airlines placing orders for fifty-five of the fifty-six aircraft completed. Pan American, American Overseas Airlines, Northwest Airlines, United Airlines, BOAC and Svensk Interkontintental Lufttrafik (the forerunner of SAS) were the operators concerned. However, in the end the Scandinavian carrier never took delivery of its four examples, which were acquired by BOAC. Structurally similar to the military variants, the civilian Stratocruisers showed many differences due to operator preferences, with varying interiors and even a variation in cabin window styles, Northwest and United opting for rectangular windows whilst the others retained the conventional round style.

Whilst the plush interiors of the airlines' Stratocruisers took passenger comfort to another level, the airliner's career was blighted throughout by engine and propeller problems. The huge Pratt & Whitney R-4360 engines were the most powerful ever fitted to airliners at that time

and kept the airlines' maintenance crews very busy. The massive 'Corncob' engine, so called because of its 28-cylinder design, arranged in four rows of seven, which gave the look of a corncob when the cowls were removed, provided 3,500 hp at take-off power, thanks to a water injection system

which boosted the output from the normal 2,650 hp. This immense power was further enhanced through the inclusion of engine superchargers, collecting spent engine exhaust-gases and concentrating them through jet-type exhaust stacks for extra thrust.

Even though plans had been set in motion some two years earlier, it was the BAHF's highly successful visit to Europe with its C-54 in 1998 that provided the organisation with sufficient interest and funds to begin its ambitious programme to restore its C-97 *Angel of Deliverance*. Finally, after much hard groundwork at Moses Lake, the aircraft was flown to Big Horn County airport at Greybull on 8 October 1998. After a flight of 2 hours and 33 minutes, it touched down safely with nothing to report other than a slightly higher fuel burn than expected, which was put down to the long

climb to cross the Rocky Mountains on the eastbound ferry.

This restoration of BAHF's C-97 will bring the number of airworthy Strats to two. Making the whole project all the more amazing, the only other operational example is flown by Hawkins & Powers Aviation Inc. in the air-tanker role. H & P has been instrumental in the project and has greatly assisted the restoration through the company's considerable experience with the type, and spares-holding that is unmatched anywhere else, which currently includes another six complete airframes

in storage in Wyoming and one in California. A shortage of C-97 nose-wheel tyres was remedied in a novel way, thanks to close co-operation with the FAA, which approved a Supplementary Type Certificate for the use of DC-8 nose wheels, to allow new 36-inch tyres to be fitted. Finally, in July 2001, following a full repaint to represent YC-97A, 45-59595, the sole example used on the Berlin Airlift, *Angel of Deliverance* departed Greybull, Wyoming on the first leg of its journey to Floyd Bennett Field, Brooklyn, New York. (*Matthias Winkler*)

Nowadays, for the most part, air travel is accepted by hundreds of thousands of passengers as very routine. However, the post-war years saw huge advances, both in aircraft design and passenger comfort. To many international long-haul operators, the choice of equipment came down to the designs of two major US manufacturers, whose designs were continuously developed to the limit of their capability, both in airframe and engine variants, to produce the epitome of long-haul air travel. Lockheed and Douglas battled to gain supremacy in this competitive market-place, reaching their zenith just as the jet age dawned. Consequently, the fruits of this hard labour were never allowed to flourish and the ultimate propliners, Douglas's DC-7C and Lockheed's L-1649 Starliner, enjoyed a very short time at the top.

This heyday of air travel is being recaptured by many ambitious and complex restoration projects around the world. This view, once common to many airline passengers, of a pair of mighty Wright R-3350s pounding at cruise power, is soon to be enjoyed once again by European enthusiasts if the ambitious plans of Swiss organisation Super

Constellation Flyers Association are realised. On 7 November 2000 the first positive signs appeared that yet another Super Constellation may soon be operational, when Super Constellation N105CF lifted off from Santo Domingo. Piloted by Captain Frank Lang and

president of the Super Constellation Flyers Association, Captain Francisco Agullo, with Carlos Gomez as flight engineer, the aircraft took flight for the first time in over three years on the first leg of its long journey to Europe.

The latest example of Lockheed's finest to be restored began life as a US Navy Model R7V-1, the military version of the L-1049B. This variant was built with forward and aft fuselage side cargo doors and heavy-duty flooring, which would help secure its later life in civilian hands, and featured a revised wing design to accept increased gross weights. Navy Super Constellations also differed from their Air Force counterparts, as well as all civilian Super Connie variants, in having round cabin windows instead of the standard rectangular style. Delivered on 28 September 1953 as Bu. No. 131636, it was accepted a few days later by Navy Logistic Support Squadron VR-8 at Hickam, Hawaii. Struck off charge on 15 June 1958 with 5,248 hours in the log, the aircraft was one of thirty-two R7V-1s modified to C-121Gs for use by the US Air Force following their retirement from naval service. Absorbed into USAF-MATS control at Moffett Field, California and allocated USAF serial 54-4062, it flew on passenger and cargo duties throughout the Pacific and Far Eastern region until reassignment

in 1963 when it moved to the 187th Air Transport Squadron of the Wyoming ANG.

This Connie's last front-line duties in the military were with the west-coast wing of the Air Force Aerospace Defense Command (ADC)'s airborne radar unit, the 552nd Airborne Early Warning and Control (AEW & C) Wing, at McClellan AFB. Seven of the converted C-121Gs were operated for transition training flights and general

logistics. In its twilight, 54-4062 was transferred yet again, this time to the 79th AEW & C Squadron at Homestead AFB in Florida, the only Air Force Reserve unit nominated by the ADC, where it was operated in a similar support role. This picture shows the aircraft wearing its AFRes markings, at rest in the 'boneyard' at Davis-Monthan during late 1982, having finally been retired four years earlier.

By the mid-1980s, the majority of the Super Constellations still remaining in storage at Davis-Monthan were specially modified EC-121s, with only a handful of airframes being 'stock' cargo variants, such as 54-4062. Consequently, this aircraft was offered for sale, for operation under civilian ownership, at one of the regular auction sales, and on 15 October 1985 local contractor DMI Aviation acquired the aircraft. Registered N2114Z, the Connie was moved to DMI's yard until a sale to Dominican Republic-based freight operator Aerochago was concluded on 31 January 1990. Given the registration HI-583CT, the aircraft joined a number of similar types that had been obtained in the same manner, which operated regular cargo flights between Santo Domingo, Aguadilla, Puerto Rico and Miami. The company ceased flying in 1993 following a downgrading of operation of Dominican-registered propeller-driven types to the USA, following investigations into operation and maintenance procedures. This move forced many operators into bankruptcy, including Aerochago, whose Super Constellations were parked up and left to the elements. HI-583CT's last flight was a training sortie in 1997.

In June 2000, the Super Constellation Flyers Association bought the aircraft and began work to have it ferried to the USA, where a full inspection and restoration could be carried out in preparation for its delivery to Europe. The aircraft required number 2 engine changed, a number of Airworthiness Directives completed on the propellers and various checks on the electrical and hydraulic systems, as it had not flown since 1997. Initial plans for a ferry flight to Avra Valley in September 2000 were delayed slightly until minor undercarriage problems were corrected at Santo Domingo and, following successful engine runs on 3 November, the Connie finally took flight again on 7 November bound, initially, for Opa Locka, Florida.

The next leg of the journey to Avra began on 4 January 2001, when a non-stop 8.5 hour flight was planned, although excessive oil consumption by number 2 engine and strong headwinds forced a landing in El Paso. However, the engine oil pressure warning light indicated the engine was running dry and a three-engine landing was successfully carried out at Conroe, Texas after 5.5 hours in the air. On Saturday 7 January, after completion of engine repairs at Conroe, the Super Constellation completed its journey to Avra Valley, Arizona. Since its arrival in Arizona, a volunteer crew from Switzerland has begun to strip the paint and start work on the cabin refurbishment. Although there is still much to be done, summer 2002 should see the completion of restoration work and a triumphant arrival of the Super Constellation at its new home in Basle not long after.

In this final chapter, many ambitious and exciting restorations of old and rare propliners have been described. However, there remains one whose story is deserving of a fitting ending. One man has dedicated much of his life to the preservation and upkeep of one particular aircraft type, a type that epitomises the ultimate development of the piston-engined airliner, the Lockheed L-1649 Starliner. Lockheed built only forty-four L-1649 Starliners, the largest, fastest and most advanced of the Constellation family. Maurice Roundy, who owns three of these magnificent airliners, has toiled, often single-handed, for the past twenty years to have a Starliner restored and returned to full airworthiness.

The fifth-from-last Constellation variant ever produced was delivered to Lufthansa in December 1957 as D-ALAN, and was immediately introduced to service on the airline's premier New York services from Germany. Starliners replaced the Super Constellations and allowed direct, non-stop flights to New York from Frankfurt and Düsseldorf, in both directions, for the first time. Their time at the top was limited, however, as by March 1960 the Starliner's major routes were taken over by the airline's first Boeing 707s. This signalled the beginning of the end for this magnificent airliner, and Lufthansa ordered the conversion of two examples to pure freight configuration whilst the remainder were relegated to secondary routes. This aircraft was leased for a while in 1962 before finally being sold in 1966, becoming N179AV with travel club Air Venturers, whose operations took the Starliner far and wide. Disposed of in 1968, it was re-registered N974R and, after having a number of subsequent owners, ended up in long-term storage in Fort Lauderdale, Florida, by 1976.

Under the name of Maine Coast Airways, Maurice Roundy acquired N974R in 1985 and began the long and difficult task of returning it to flight status. Two memorable attempts to ferry the Starliner north to his base in Maine, where his other two L-1649s are resident, ended with a forced landing at Sanford, Florida in September 1988. Undaunted, Maurice set to with determination to bring the Starliner back to flight status, and continued its restoration, often single-handed, until July 2001, when he announced it was ready to fly once more. With an FAA 'permit to fly" issued, and a more appropriate home at Kermit Weeks's Fantasy of Flight, N974R took flight on 19 October for an eventful but successful 45-minute flight from Sanford to Polk City and an altogether more secure future.

The number of airworthy Lockheed Constellations is set to increase when this example takes flight later this year, following its lengthy restoration. The aircraft, part of USAF's original batch of C-121As and sister ship to the well known MATS Connie, is owned by Stichting Constellation Nederland (SCN) and is part of the ambitious 'Connie Comeback' programme started by the Dutch National Aviodome Museum to restore and fly the aircraft to the Netherlands for display at the Aviodome Museum site. The Constellation holds a special significance in Holland, where KLM Royal Dutch Airlines began operating the type in November 1946, in the form of the original L-049. The following year Model 749s, similar to this, joined the fleet, which would eventually number forty-eight different aircraft, of both standard and Super Constellations variants, over a period of sixteen years.

Last operated as a bud-worm sprayer with Conifer Aviation at St Jean, Quebec, registered C-GXKR, the Connie was withdrawn from service in 1980 and stored at Mont Joli, awaiting sale. In March 1988 the Dutch Association of Constellation Enthusiasts was formed and, following extended negotiations, C-GXKR's sale to the SCN was eventually concluded in 1993 and so began the lengthy and expensive task of its restoration. In September 1993 the aircraft was ferried from Canada to Tucson, Arizona where restoration would eventually be carried out, under the guidance of Vern Raburn's Constellation Group at Avra Valley. Registered N749VR, the Connie remained grounded at Avra, donating parts to the MATS Connie until work began in earnest in March 2001 when the first team of volunteers from the Aviodome arrived in Tucson to begin work. By September 2001 things were progressing well, with the airframe stripped and repainted, a replacement short nose had been fitted and all essential work on engines and systems was reaching completion. However, damage to number 4 engine during run-up checks delayed the post-restoration flight date until spring 2002.

Summer 2002 should see the triumphant arrival in Holland of the 'Comeback Connie', the culmination of much hard work and enthusiasm by the dedicated team at SCN and the Aviodome.

It is heartening to see the continued increase in numbers of airworthy propliners throughout the world, operated either privately or commercially. Air-tanker operators in Canada and the USA are to be congratulated for the continued existence of so many ageing propliners, including this pristine example, which was recently fully restored in preparation for the 2002 season by its owners, Aero-Flite. Featured earlier in this book, the C-54 had been retired from fire-fighting and its retardant tanks removed in the early 1990s by another operator, who restored its original military olive-drab markings. The aircraft remained in this condition until mid-2001 when Aero-Flite began its restoration to air-tanker status.

Aero-Flite's immaculate fleet of Douglas C-54s have benefited from the popular practice of applying period colour schemes during restoration, having now all received the tasteful and stylish markings of their manufacturer.

INDEX

Avro Anson 87, 88

Boeing 247 15
Boeing 367 Stratofreighter 104, 105
Boeing 377 Stratocruiser 106

Convair 340/440 75–82
Curtis-Wright C-46 61–3

De Havilland DH-104 Dove 90
De Havilland DH-89 Dragon Rapide 83–5
De Havilland DH-114 Heron 90
De Havilland Australia DHA-3 Drover 91–2
Douglas DC-2 16–8
Douglas DC-3 19–37
Douglas DC-4 38–60, 111

Douglas DC-6 93–7
Douglas DC-7 98–102

Ford Tri-motor 13–14

Junkers Ju-52 5–13

Lockheed Constellation 107–10

Martin 4-0-4 63–74

Scottish Aviation Twin Pioneer 89
Short Sandringham 86
Stinson SM-6000 Tri-motor 14

Vickers Viscount 103

Airliners from the 1930s to the 1960s

The walk across the apron, the steep climb up the boarding stairs, the smile of the welcoming stewardess and then at last – the thunder as the piston engines begin to spin the great props to a vanishing point. This was air travel in the early years, after World War II. It was an age in which the piston aero-engine reached its zenith and every type of aircraft had its own distinctive features. Now, in an age when space-age design and technology have led to much uniformity, air travel has become almost boring by comparison with that of yesteryear.

This book celebrates those remaining classic airliners that have been lovingly restored in order that the joy of early air travel can be recreated and celebrated once more.

Airlife
www.airlifebooks.com

£12.99UK $19.95US

ISBN 1-84037-274-5